Advance Praise for Million Dollar Family Secrets

There are very few things that we can learn in life that are as important as learning how to invest. In other words, how do we make our money work for us instead of working for our money our entire lives? If you are serious—not curious—about learning how to make your money work for you, then Kiana is definitely the teacher, the guide, and the author for you. Read this book, study this book, and practice the principles in this book. Your life and your family's life will be better for it. Congratulations in advance.

—**Myron Golden**, Bestselling Author of *From the Trash Man to the Cash Man* and *B.O.S.S. Moves*

Listen. I hate math, but this book will change your life. It's SO GOOD, I made it required reading for my kids. They got it right away, and started investing. Like, WHAT? They are in middle school. Thank you for changing our family's life, Kiana!!

—**Eileen Wilder**, Bestselling Author and Host of The Confident Closer® Show

I can divide my life into two parts: When I worked for my money and when I learned to make my money work for me. I used to dread money management because I didn't know what I was doing. Thanks to Kiana, I now have specific strategies that work for me, tailored to my goals and personality. This book is a must-read for all women, and, with any luck, will become mandatory reading in schools. What Kiana teaches is the new "home economics" that women need. This no-fluff book makes investing easy to follow—and it's laid out in simple steps that anyone can understand. Do yourself a favor and read this book, make notes, and grab a second copy for a friend!

—**Carla White**, Founder & CEO of Hiro.fm

MILLION DOLLAR FAMILY

Secrets

Make Your Money Work for You to Create Generational Wealth

KIANA DANIAL

MILLION DOLLAR FAMILY SECRETS
Make Your Money Work for You to Create Generational Wealth

Copyright © 2022. Kiana Danial. All rights reserved. No part of this publication may be reproduced, distributed, or transmitted in any form or by any means, including photocopying, recording, or other electronic or mechanical methods, without the prior written permission of the publisher, except in the case of brief quotations embodied in critical reviews and certain other noncommercial uses permitted by copyright law. For permission requests, speaking inquiries, and bulk order purchase options, email support@investdiva.com.

Invest Diva
PO Box 611
Westport, CT 06881
InvestDiva.com

Paperback ISBN: 978-1-7374553-7-0
eBook ISBN: 978-1-7374553-8-7

Cover and Interior Design by Transcendent Publishing
Edited by Lori Lynn Enterprises
Cover Design Concept by Tristan Craig
Cover Outfit Styling by Hannah Spencer, Wardrobe Stylist
Cover Photo by Keyvan Behpour
Timeline Mountain Infographic by Yellow Duck/Shutterstock.com
Red Horizontal Waving Flag Infographic by Topuria Design/Shutterstock.com

All information provided is for general informational and educational purposes only and does not constitute investment advice. The information contained in this book is intended to be truthful and not misleading, as required by FTC regulations. INVESTDIVA.COM, Kiana Danial, and KPHR Capital, LLC are not registered or licensed as investment advisors with the SEC. INVESTDIVA.COM, Kiana Danial, and KPHR Capital, LLC do not offer personalized investment advice. Only your registered/licensed financial advisor can give you personalized investment advice. INVESTDIVA.COM, Kiana Danial, and KPHR Capital, LLC and its affiliates are not licensed/registered to make, and do not offer, personalized investment or financial advice as defined by the SEC. Investing involves substantial risk. Results are not guaranteed.

Printed in the United States of America

Dedication

To my daughter Jasmine who keeps giving me purpose.

Contents

Foreword ix

Introduction xi
   From Welfare Diva to Millionaire Diva

Chapter One 1
   What Is a Millionaire?

Chapter Two 13
   Learn the Facts—and Myths—About Your Money

Chapter Three 31
   Learn the Easiest, Low-Risk Way to Start Controlling Your Money Right Now

Chapter Four 41
   Learn How to Accelerate Your Portfolio

Chapter Five 55
   Create an Account with a Broker/Exchange

Chapter Six 65
   Figure Out Where You Stand Financially

Chapter Seven 71
   Clarify Your Financial Goals

Chapter Eight 83
   Go Asset Picking

Chapter Nine 89
  Create a Unique Investment Strategy Based on Your Risk Tolerance and Financial Goals

Chapter Ten 95
  Follow the "No-Math" Investing Method

Chapter Eleven 101
  Learn the Art of Buying Low and Selling High

Chapter Twelve 111
  Apply the "No-Time" Investing Method

Chapter Thirteen 119
  Use the Zen Wealth Generator to Compound Your Money Year after Year

Chapter Fourteen 131
  Increase Your Income

Chapter Fifteen 143
  Increase Your Influence

Chapter Sixteen 159
  Create an Automated Active Income

Chapter Seventeen 177
  Create Generational Wealth

Acknowledgments 189

About the Author 193

How to Get More Help 197

FOREWORD

I designed the world's fastest helicopter ... I led AI for the world's largest defense contractor ... I solve complicated problems for a living. I don't have a lot of free time, so I never learned how to invest to build wealth.

I was leaving my money with corporate "for-profit" money managers, but it became clear they didn't care about my portfolio.

In my experience, the only person that truly cares about your portfolio is you, so I decided to get educated and take control of my finances.

Invest Diva has helped me learn how to build wealth in a way that is fun and easy to understand. I've been in the program for a while now, and over that time, I've been able to leverage the techniques that Kiana teaches to help grow my portfolio, and in her words, "make my money work for me."

It can be a little daunting at the start, but once you get the hang of it, you wish you had learned about it earlier. For me, it was refreshing to learn that it wasn't rocket science. In a word, it has been outstanding. Kiana makes it easy.

—Matt Tarascio
Former Chief Data & Analytics Officer and Vice President of Artificial Intelligence for Lockheed Martin

Introduction

> You've got to tell your money what to do or it will leave.

— Dave Ramsey

From Welfare Diva to Millionaire Diva

*I*t was a year after I had left Tokyo for New York City, and it felt like I finally had it all: a dream job on Wall Street, a boyfriend, and an apartment on the Upper East Side—just like what I had seen in the movies and on TV in shows like *Gossip Girl*, *Sex and the City*, and *Friends*.

It was 2011, and I was living the life of Alicia Keys in *New York* … *"Concrete jungle where dreams are made of…"*

Little did I know, things were about to change.

On a day I thought I had achieved an amazing performance, I got fired. A few days later, my boyfriend dumped me. Soon after, I ran out of money to pay rent.

It wasn't the first time I had hit rock bottom throughout my journey from Iran, to Japan, to the United States. But it felt like the worst one.

I had always thought, *by the time I'm 27 I will have all things figured out.*

I had just tasted what it feels like to have it all … and BAM. Just like that, it was all taken away from me.

What are my parents going to think? What are people going to say? Where am I going to live? What if no one will ever love me? I felt like a failure. Again.

For the longest time, I told potential employers that I had quit my job because it was way too embarrassing to admit I had gotten fired. Regardless, I wasn't able to find a new job.

Even though I had studied Electrical Engineering for seven years in Japan, I knew I didn't want to work as an engineer. Studying it in Japanese (the language I started learning when I moved from Iran to Japan just before turning 19) basically resulted in me not understanding anything. I barely graduated college.

And I still wasn't proficient in English, my third language.

Deep down, I suspected they knew (and later found out those prospective employers *did* know) that I had gotten fired from my Wall Street Job.

Unemployable, I thought to myself. Too heartbroken to make rational relationship decisions, I now had a new problem: a falling out with my family.

WAKE UP!!!

It was as if my alter ego was shaking my shoulders. I suddenly realized I was falling into an old habit—the old habit that had me falling down to rock bottom time and time again in the past.

It's the one that was driving me into a welfare house. It's my…

Welfare Diva mentality.

I had to snap out of it before I fell lower. I needed to go back to the basic principles:

- Who are you?

- Do you truly believe you deserve wealth?

- What is your ability to act in spite of fear, in spite of worry, in spite of inconvenience, in spite of discomfort?

- Can you act when you are not in the mood?

I remembered reading that most people who have "blown up" financially lose it all in no time. Or they have excellent opportunities to start, and start well, but then they go down.

I was becoming a statistic.

While I was trying to blame my misfortune—my drop from the top to the bottom—on "bad luck," "a horrible boss," and a "lousy boyfriend" ...

The real reason could only be found within ME. I had fallen back into the pattern I inherited from the generations before me. That is why every time I've come into big money and happiness, it's been short-lived and I've lost it.

We see this over and over again with lottery winners. Seventy percent of lottery winners LOSE all of their money and end up bankrupt just a few years after receiving a large payout. Why is that?

The vast majority of people simply don't have the internal capacity to create and hold onto large amounts of money. They are not prepared to face the increased challenges that go with more money and success.

In the case of lottery winners, research shows that regardless of the size of their winnings, most lottery winners eventually return to their original financial state and the amount they can comfortably handle.

It suddenly became clear to me: I had fallen down to rock bottom—yet again—because deep down I didn't think I deserved the "Upper East Side" luxury living.

It's time to snap out of it forever. It's time to become a …

Millionaire Diva.

In this book, I take you through my journey of transformation from a Welfare Diva to a Millionaire Diva, how I've helped thousands of my students along the way to achieve similar results, and how I can help YOU.

If you would like to see some examples of how we've helped our Invest Diva Community, I've collected screenshots from our students celebrating their success, #DivaWins, with our program. Please visit:

InvestDivaReviews.com

INTRODUCTION

My personal portfolio, which I've personally been managing for the past six years, has just hit a total of $5,254,399.55 at the time of this writing. This amount only includes the earnings and profits I gained using a system I call the Zen Wealth Generator™ which helped me build a Diva Wealth Ecosystem. You'll learn more about that later.

As I have achieved financial freedom and early retirement, which means I don't have to work ever again, you may be asking, "Why are you still working?"

The answer is simple: to help others.

Once you achieve everything you've ever dreamed of in life, and have made sure your family is set up, you become addicted to sharing your journey and helping as many people as possible achieve the same results.

Personally, my goal is to help one million moms take control of their financial future by the year 2025. If my team and I end up helping additional millions of dads, aunts, uncles, entrepreneurs, engineers, immigrants, double-black-diamond skiers, or any other type of awesome humans, sign us up!

We're here to help you take control of your financial future. It's what we call the Invest Diva Movement.

I JUST MADE MY FIRST $1,000!!!

I'm never keeping money in the bank again.

I'm so EXCITED that I'm screaming with JOY!!!

This is just the beginning and so excited to learn more!!

—Angelica O.

Chapter One

>

Being rich is having money;
being wealthy is
having time.

— *Margaret Bonnano*

What Is a Millionaire?

The title of this book is *Million Dollar Family Secrets*, so I think it's fair to define what a millionaire really is. Unfortunately, in our culture today, millionaires are getting a bad rap. Entrepreneurs and millionaires are constantly being vilified by the media, who often attempt to point the current economic problems on those who have made it out of the rat race.

While there is a real economic problem in our society today, unfortunately, the wrong type of people are getting vilified. As a result, there's a very negative mindset about having money.

My three-year-old toddler has been obsessed with a "girl empowerment" children's show called *Rainbow Rangers*. It focuses on seven 9-year-old girls who are the guardians of both nature and their land. I was, at first, very excited for my daughter to watch this show because it shows her how powerful girls can be.

But as I watched a few episodes, I noticed that the series' villain is always a millionaire entrepreneur.

They vilify this millionaire and his daughter with terms like "greedy" and "selfish" on almost every episode of this children's show.

On the surface, this may sound like a noble education, but if you dig deeper, you'll notice that the vilification of millionaires starts very early. The millionaire characters are almost always the bad, greedy guys who are trying to destroy things. The heroes are the poor, the orphans, and the "have-nots."

What message is this sending to our children?

"If you want to be a hero, you shall not care about money. You shall not become a millionaire."

As if being a millionaire and a good person are mutually exclusive. As if you cannot be both wealthy AND a hero.

You have picked up this book, so I'm guessing there is a part of you that wants to become a millionaire. But if there is even a shred of uncertainty or doubt that becoming a millionaire is going to turn you into a "villain," chances are you are going to subconsciously do things to prevent you from achieving that goal.

Before I reveal the different types of millionaires, let me make something clear that is far more important …

Money doesn't *make* you a good or a bad person. Money is just a tool. All it does is *amplify* who you truly are.

If someone is inherently stingy, mean, or ill-spirited, having more money will simply amplify that. If they're helpful, generous, considerate, charitable, and positive, becoming a millionaire will echo their good vibes. Money is a magnifier. It doesn't change you. It reveals you.

CHAPTER ONE

By becoming a millionaire, you can become the change you've always wanted to see in the world.

So before we get deeper into this book to reveal the methods that I used to make my millions, please promise that you will only use this book for good.

Promise?

Great! Now you have my permission to move forward.

Is Becoming a Millionaire Important?

When we talk about millionaires, it is important to understand how vastly different they are from billionaires. A billion is a THOUSAND million. A huge misconception a lot of people have when they think about money is that all wealthy people have similar circumstances. They confuse being a millionaire with living a Jeff Bezos kind of life. Jeff Bezos has so much money that spending $2.9 million feels the same to him as the average American spending $2.

A millionaire does NOT live the same type of life as a billionaire. Millionaires are comfortable and can provide well for their families, along with leaving a solid financial legacy.

A millionaire in our day and age lives a similar life to a middle-class corporate manager back in the '70s. Millionaire status shouldn't feel outside your reach. If you want the ease that comes with having more than enough, then it's important that you aspire to become a millionaire.

If you're making less than $10K per month right now, I know something about you:

You're struggling financially.

How do I know that?

Because there's something you want to do that you can't do.

Maybe it's hiring a full-time nanny so you can stop going insane with your constant parenting.

Maybe it's taking a nice vacation.

Maybe it's giving to a charity that really moves your heart.

Maybe it's paying for your kids' college.

Maybe it's helping with an aging parent.

If you've hit $10K per month and plateaued, then you're financially challenged.

You can do some of the things that you want to do, but you can't do all of them.

I know this because I was there, sitting at below $10K per month until a couple of years ago.

My husband is an actual rocket scientist, and he makes a good salary, but when we first had our daughter, we struggled!

The hospital sent us a bill we literally couldn't afford to pay and insurance somehow didn't cover it, so our finances were maxed out. We were under tremendous stress.

I remember what it was like to struggle at $12K per month. Because when you first start making $10K, you adjust your lifestyle. Then, if you're not careful—and you don't follow some of the principles I'm going to teach you in this book—you can become financially challenged at a higher level.

Do you know how many high-level entrepreneurs I know who make $1 million per year but are more broke than a college student with a part-time job at McDonald's?

This is because wealth is a side effect of financial literacy, not the other way around. If you want to become a millionaire, you need to get your fundamentals right.

The Four Types of Millionaires

Not all millionaires are created equal. There is a type that you want to avoid at all costs, and that is what I call an *Imaginary Millionaire*. This is the type of millionaire who **makes** $1 million but spends it all. They don't let it work and compound, and at the end of the day, they're actually broke.

The *real* millionaires typically fall under one, if not all, of the categories below:

1. Asset Millionaire

An asset millionaire is someone whose net worth is over $1 million.

Net worth = assets - liabilities

Assets include cash, investments, real property (land and permanent structures, such as homes attached to the property), and personal property (everything else that you own, such as cars, boats, furniture, and jewelry).

Liabilities include all of your outstanding debts including but not limited to:

- Car loan(s)
- Home equity loan
- Margin loans
- Mortgage
- Rental real estate mortgage
- Second mortgage
- Vacation or second home mortgage
- Credit card debt
- Medical bills
- Personal loans
- Student loans
- Other debt and outstanding bills

If you subtract your liabilities (debts) from your assets and end up with a number larger than $1 million, congrats! You're an asset millionaire!

2. Cash Flow Millionaire

A cash flow millionaire is someone who makes $1M+ per day, per month, or per year. Cash flow millionaire status can be achieved through passive income such as rental income, automated business income, and/or dividends. It can also be achieved through *automated active income* like my webinar funnel that I talk about in Chapter 16 that makes my family a minimum of $500K per month without me being involved.

3. Portfolio Millionaire

This level of millionaire gets you one step closer to actual financial freedom. I explain the exact formula for financial freedom in the final chapter of this book so you can calculate your unique number. But for now, just know that a portfolio millionaire is someone who has an investment portfolio (an accumulated of online assets such as stocks or cryptocurrencies) where the realized + unrealized capital gains are over $1 million.

Some people mistake a portfolio millionaire with a *Liquid Millionaire*. A Liquid Millionaire is someone who has $1 million in the bank. As we will discuss in the next chapter, keeping all your money in the bank is not the best strategy for your financial future.

4. Trust Fund Millionaire

The fourth type of millionaire is where it's at! This is where you need to aim to be. That is what John D. Rockefeller meant when he stated, "Own nothing, but control everything."

This is the fundamental rule of asset protection that many people forget about. Once you become any of the previous three types of millionaires, it is important to look into asset protection. It's part of the Financial Accounting Standards Board (FASB) rules. These rules govern all CPAs and other accountants. It doesn't take much effort to search for the right people to set up legal protections, so take a little bit of time to protect your assets. That way, you'll be able to keep the money you make through thick and thin.

So what type of a millionaire should you aspire to become?

The answer is, all of the above!

I know what you might be thinking right now.

"But Kiana, that's too hard!"

So I have no choice but to quote Henry Ford:

> **"If you believe you can, or if you believe you can't, you're right."**

I have learned over years and years of hustling my butt off, learning everything there is about any topic I thought could make me money, that …

CHAPTER ONE

Believing that you can achieve something is infinitely more important than knowing how to do it.

When I say "belief," I mean "a well-rounded expectation about the future." This will help you think differently so that you can achieve different things.

Can you agree that if you keep doing what you're doing right now, you will achieve the same exact results you have so far?

Albert Einstein said the definition of insanity is "doing the same thing over and over again and expecting a different result."

I want to add to Albert Einstein and say that your expectation of a favorable outcome is the only thing that is going to give you the ability to take an action that moves your life forward.

That's because you believe anything you tell yourself, even if you're lying. Let me give you an example …

My mom and sister are some of the most anxious people I know. Growing up, every time I went out, my mom sat paralyzed in a chair, anxious that I was going to get hit by a car.

I never got hit by a car.

But what happened to my mom instead was that half of her hair fell out, she was too anxious to do anything for herself, and now, at an old age, she's getting every sickness known to man.

She's had numerous types of cancer, and every year the doctors discover a new (nongenetic) disease.

These were all the outcomes of her imagination because she believed what she told herself.

How would you make decisions differently if you actually believed—and were certain—that it's possible to have a million-dollar portfolio—even if you're super busy? If beliefs are just stories you make up about the future, then what if you believed you could become a millionaire?

You believe anything you tell yourself.

If beliefs are stories that you make up about the future, why don't you tell yourself better stories that will enable you to make better decisions, so that you can achieve better results?

Chapter Two

> The stock market
> is filled with individuals
> who know the price of everything,
> but the value of nothing.
>
> —Philip A. Fisher

Learn the Facts—and Myths—
About Your Money

I was earning peanuts for being a participant in a Japanese social debate series on Japan's National TV when the 2008 global market crash happened.

I didn't know anything about money or how to manage the money I was earning. So my money was just sitting there in a bank in Japan. I didn't even care about it at that point because, throughout my upbringing, I was taught that money isn't even important.

And then it happened: a massive global economic recession. Businesses were going bankrupt and people were losing their jobs. We were talking about this on my TV show when one of the panelists said, "The governments are printing money to save the economy."

He asked me, "Do you know what this means?"

Reluctantly, I shrugged my shoulders and said, "No."

What he said next is what inspired my whole switch from electrical engineering to finance.

He said, "This means that leaving your money in the bank is

actually like setting your money on fire …" He went on to explain that when the government prints money to bail out corporations and give stimulus checks, inflation goes higher.

Inflation, which is the reason why your parents paid way less for a gallon of milk than you do, is designed to lower the value of your money every year, so every moment that your money is sitting in the bank, you're losing money.

When I heard that I thought, *Oh my gosh! I've got to do something with my money that's just sitting in the bank so it won't lose its value to inflation!*

But I knew nothing about money, I sucked at math, I was barely surviving college, and I had no idea how to do these things.

I asked around a little bit and found out the best thing I could do was to find a money manager to manage my money for me and invest it on my behalf. That had to be better than having it just sitting in the bank. And I thought it was definitely better than me doing it on my own.

I soon found a money management company that was based in the UK and who had an operating branch in Tokyo. The money manager, Tim, talked to me about all the funds their high-level analysts were managing. He used many intimidating words that got me more confused on how they do things, and at the same time, more convinced that I knew nothing about finance and I should hand him my money right away.

I thought the money management company with all their fancy C-level titles like CFP, CMT, and CFA had my best interests in mind. I mean, that's their job, right?

CHAPTER TWO

As it turned out ... not so much. This brings us to Myth Number 1.

Myth NO. 1

Money managers have my best interest at heart.

Years later, when I started working at a brokerage firm on Wall Street, I learned that they had THEIR best interest in mind. Instead of investing in what was going to make ME money, they invested my money in stuff that made THEM more money. They got commissions from the partners, brokers, and companies they invested my money in.

On top of that, they were taking a commission on what little money I did make.

So, what money managers typically do is take your money and put it into something called a mutual fund. Now don't worry about what that means, just know that ...

Mutual funds UNDERPERFORM the market average by 86%!

The market average is around 8% to 12% per year. They UNDERPERFORM compared to that average, which means my money was barely growing.

Money managers, who are supposed to be good at investing, actually lose money compared to the market average.

A few years later, when I got fired from my Wall Street job, I really needed that money back to pay rent. It was right around the time my boyfriend dumped me and I had the falling out with my family.

Then, I suddenly remembered! *I have money in that money manager's account. After all these years, it has probably grown into something substantial! That's going to help me out of this misery so I can at least find a place to live.*

So I called up my money manager, Tim, and said, "Hey, I recently lost my job, and I need money to pay rent ... Can you please help me pull my money out of the fund?"

He said, "Sure ... but you need to pay a 75% penalty because you're taking it out early."

"What?! Do you remember telling me I could take the money out anytime I want before I invested with you guys?!"

He said, "Well, yes ... you certainly can take it out. You simply need to pay a penalty for taking it out early. You agreed to this on page 13 of the 28-page agreement you signed."

Of course I did. I had blindly signed an agreement simply because I was too excited to start investing my money with someone I thought I could trust and who had my best interest at heart.

A 75% penalty for withdrawing early means that if you put in $100,000, you'd come out with $25,000.

Great investment, right? Not so much.

The money management company soon stopped communicating with me and then said that Tim had left the firm.

I was really angry. I felt defeated and manipulated. So I promised myself I would never put my financial future in someone else's hands.

Don't ever put your entire financial future in someone else's hands.

I told myself, *Enough is enough. I'm going to take things into my own hands.* I became obsessed with learning about finance and wealth. I started interning for free in small financial firms to learn different investing strategies. I studied for the CFP and CMT and CFA—all these fancy certified financial titles the money managers had.

I went through the courses, gleaning all the knowledge, but I didn't actually take the final exams to become certified. If I had, then I would have had to follow their regulations. That would have restricted me from educating people on social media venues, and my goal is to educate people to become their *own* CFPs.

I also started investing on my own and documented my trading journey in my first book, which ended up getting published by McGraw-Hill.

I then decided to help more people who were intimidated by the whole financial world. I founded the Invest Diva Movement and **learn.investdiva.com** to help thousands of people take control of their financial future.

Now, my money is growing from anywhere between 12% to 245% per year with minimal effort on my end. This means I don't have to rely on money managers, I'm not losing money to inflation in the bank, and I'm not even relying on my husband (find out how we met in the About the Author section at the end of this book).

I'm in control of my financial future no matter what life throws at me. This has given me a huge sense of peace of mind.

Banking vs. Money Managers vs. Investing

Leaving your money in the bank is like buying a Chanel bag or a new car.

When you put money in the bank, the value depreciates every day. It's like buying a new Chanel bag or a brand new car. That car loses half of its value the moment it comes out of the dealership, and the bag becomes less valuable every day as it sits in your closet. Your money is the same way in the bank.

Giving your money to a money manager is like handing your new car or Chanel bag to your teenager.

Even worse than leaving your money in the bank is giving your money to a money manager. This is like handing your new Chanel bag or car to the teenage neighbor!

Imagine you bought a new Chanel bag, and you let your teenager neighbor borrow it to go to a nasty bar in your new car. She drunk-drives her way back home and then demands a bunch of money to return your bag and car back to you!

When you use a money manager, all of your hard-earned money is tied up with someone who doesn't have your best interests in mind, and then they charge you for it, too!

Investing is like buying a limited-edition Hermès bag or Lamborghini and selling it for more money.

When you invest your money by yourself, it's like buying a limited edition Hermès bag or a Lamborghini and then selling it on eBay to a luxury brand collector or a car fanatic for even more money.

Myth NO. 2

If I make more money, I'll be wealthy!

This is by far the biggest money myth out there, especially among entrepreneurs. It wasn't too long ago that my friend Mark was receiving his Two Comma Club Award at Funnel Hacking LIVE …

He was standing in line with a fellow Two Comma Club Award Winner, only to find out that their company had filed for bankruptcy a week prior to the event.

Unfortunately, this is not that uncommon among high-performing entrepreneurs who generate seven-figure revenues.

Many high-performing, 7-figure entrepreneurs go bankrupt.

Many of these entrepreneurs spend all of their budgets on ads and mismanage the revenue they're generating. So much so that when it comes to their net income, they actually end up in the negative, and as a result, they need to file for bankruptcy or shut down their business altogether.

Unfortunately, our school systems fail us in so many ways with money and financial literacy. As a result, most people aren't aware of the fact that:

Financial literacy isn't a side effect of wealth … Wealth is a side effect of financial literacy.

In other words, if you can't manage $100, you can't manage $100,000.

If I hand you $1 million today, but you don't know how to manage it, and if you don't have a Millionaire Diva mindset, you are likely going to spend your way back to your comfort zone of being a Welfare Diva.

In fact, evidence shows that most people who make it to the top 1 percent of income earners usually don't stay at the top for very long.

The psychology behind this could be the same reason why the

majority of lottery winners file for bankruptcy within three to five years.

This could also be a result of the wrong money mindset. If you have a Welfare Diva (broke) mindset, chances are, you'll unintentionally mismanage your money to go back to your natural comfort zone of being broke.

Myth NO. 3

My spouse (or some other family member) will take care of me.

This myth is especially (and unfortunately) common among women, and one of the reasons why I'm so passionate about empowering women to take control of their financial future with the Invest Diva Movement.

I'm not meaning to scare you, but the reality is that the average age of widowhood is just 59. Women live longer in general. This means that women need more money for retirement. I once published a TikTok about this and some of the comments shocked me. Most said that even if they outlive their spouse, the life insurance will be there for them. One of my followers went so far as to say, "A woman's retirement fund doubles once her husband dies."

While there's some truth to this, here's the first reason why your spouse's (or other family member's) financial status doesn't guarantee your financial well-being …

When someone's family member dies, no matter how much money they inherit, they are going to get hit by trauma.

In that state of mind, they're not going to be able to learn how to manage their money!

And as we pointed out in Myth Number 1, money managers typically don't have their clients' best interests at heart. In many cases, they actually TAKE ADVANTAGE of the mourner.

As David Bach, the author of *Smart Women Finish Rich,* puts it ...

"It's neither safe nor practical to assume that the man in your life can be counted on to take care of your finances."

Even ultra-rich people aren't immune to this. For example, Kobe Bryant's wife inherited millions after Kobe's tragic death, but unless she was on top of his finances prior to his passing, she wouldn't have been fully aware of the extent of her husband's holdings and interests. When Kobe passed, she probably didn't even want to think about money because she was so shaken with grief.

That means she was vulnerable.

Assuming many advisors and partners were involved, there's a strong chance that they didn't act in her best interest and may have taken advantage of her while she was heartbroken and mourning. Being ultra rich doesn't protect you from tragedy, scammers, or potential financial ruin.

Lady Gaga is another example. She's the type of artist who doesn't invest at all. As a result, she went bankrupt and was $3 million in debt after her Monster Ball tour.

Meanwhile, we hear stories of a cab driver who started investing early and finished off with millions in her bank account all thanks to compounding—which is what we'll be discussing in Chapter 13.

As you can probably see so far, there is NO REASON you shouldn't be taking control of your money right now, and the sooner you accept this reality, the better off you will be!

Myth NO. 4

My employer-sponsored retirement account is enough.

Many of my *Make Your Money Work For You PowerCourse* students first come to me saying, "Kiana, I'm already investing. I have a 401(k) from my job."

That's great and certainly better than not investing at all. But do you know where your investments actually go when you have a 401(k)?

They go right into mutual funds. Now, if you will remember from Myth Number 1 about money managers, mutual funds actually underperform the average growth in the market.

That means your 401(k), 403(k), or any other managed retirement fund will hardly give you ANY return even after 10, 20, or 30 years.

Another big risk here is if the market crashes around the time you're ready to take that money out, you'll actually end up LOSING money inside your 401(k).

And on top of that, if you need to take your money out early for whatever reason, you'll have to pay a penalty for withdrawing the money early …

So keeping ALL your investments just in your 401(k) is, once again, locking your money in a place that's completely out of your control and at the mercy of someone else who, 96% of the time, won't even match the market average.

Did you know that …

Americans lose $5.7 billion each year to 401(k) and IRA early withdrawal fees.

This statistic is for people who are at least doing SOMETHING with their money. The rest of the people who have their money in the bank are not doing anything with it, which is worse. They're scared of investing because they think it's too risky.

The fact is that NOT investing your money is riskier because your money will be losing its value to inflation, and on top of that, you're missing out on compounding your money.

This begs the question: Who do you think benefits when you

don't invest your money and you keep it in your bank?

The answer is: The bank!

And this brings us to Myth Number 5.

Myth NO. 5

My money is safe in the bank.

Unfortunately, the majority of people who are too scared of investing their money on their own think their money will be safer in the bank.

In my *Million Dollar Family™ Accelerator* program, I'm frequently shocked to see students who've been keeping north of half a million dollars right there in their savings account.

Here are a few things people don't account for:

Inflation

The cold-hearted truth is that the government doesn't have inflation under control, and inflation is public enemy number one.

With every distress in our economy—like the 2008 global financial crisis and the 2020 COVID-19 pandemic—the Federal Reserve goes back to printing money out of thin air.

Unfortunately, for the money in your bank account, this means that it's losing its value day after day.

If your money isn't keeping up with inflation, which is MUCH higher than the tiny interest the bank pays you …

Your future is going to be expensive.

Underinsurance

What the majority of people with savings accounts don't know is that banks only insure your money up to $250,000.

In other words, if you have over $250,000 in your bank account, your money is underinsured. If the economy crashes and you need to get that money out, chances are you are never going to see that money again.

Lack of Cash

Have you ever noticed that you can't simply show up at a bank and cash out a big chunk of money? Why do you think that is?

Well, it's because banks typically don't hold more than a certain amount of cash in their vaults. And the reason for that should make you angry:

The banks are investing your money without your knowledge and reaping the benefits.

That's why they give you credit instead of actual cash, because most of your money is out there making more money for your bank, while they're out there encouraging people NOT to invest and calling it "risky" because THEY benefit when you don't invest!

Okay, okay, they give you a tiny bit of interest back in return. But that is nothing compared to what they are making at their headquarters with YOUR money!

While you should be making your money work for you (and in this book, I'm going to show you the exact steps to do so), THEY are making YOUR money work for THEM!

Doesn't this make you angry? It makes me so angry.

There is NO REASON you shouldn't be taking control of your money right now, and the sooner you accept this reality, the better off you will be—just like the thousands of our Invest Divas and Invest Divos who have learned how to make their money work for them.

The strategies in this book have helped countless Invest Divas and Invest Divos create investment strategies that are perfect for their risk tolerance and financial situation to 10X and even 100X their initial investment without spending too much time and without doing any math.

Mystie is one of our first Invest Divas to quickly multiply her investment after joining our *Make Your Money Work For You PowerCourse*.

Mystie's life turned upside down when she was diagnosed with Lyme disease. But she didn't let that take over her life. Instead, she decided to show her money who's boss, started her Invest Diva journey, and was able to 10X her initial investment in just 18 short months.

Melissa, a single mom with no prior financial education, was able to become financially independent through her Invest Diva journey. She literally knew nothing about finance or money when she started, and now she's able to support herself and her son without relying on her narcissistic ex-husband. She has been growing her money year after year.

Seeing our students take control of their financial future and make their money work for them really warms my heart. You can do this, too. If you implement these tactics in your life or your family's life, you should see results just like our other student success stories.

Chapter Three

>

The reason you
have to have a job
is because your money
is unemployed.

— Myron Golden

Learn the Easiest, Low-Risk Way to Start Controlling Your Money Right Now

When I first tell people that they should be investing, the first thing that they usually say to me is, "But Kiana, isn't investing risky?!"

If you've ever heard stories about how somebody lost a bunch of money on a meme stock, you'll probably relate to this.

After getting fired and finding out I couldn't touch the money I had in my Money Manager's account, I started hustling and learning how to trade through self-education and interning for small financial firms.

I also took some classes on reading off a teleprompter which helped me get a gig as a freelance reporter at the New York Stock Exchange (NYSE) on Wall Street. At this point, I was dying to dive into the markets and start making my money work for me …

Like I'm sure you might be right now.

Since I was only learning but didn't have much experience trading, I wasn't really confident in my choices. But, what I did have going for me was that I was surrounded by all of the best traders and investors out there while I was reporting at the New York Stock Exchange.

So naturally, I was watching what other people were doing, and making my choices based on what these world-class traders were modeling. I would interview them, take notes for myself, and apply what they said to my own trading account.

I eventually gained some confidence and went all-in with my savings of $15,000 that I had worked my butt off to accumulate. I was so excited to start growing that account and finally feel financially secure again.

Well, that didn't get me too far … I kept following what everyone else was saying to do and following the market noise. So can you guess what happened?

I lost my entire savings in one trade.

I was so upset and disappointed in myself. I mean, how could I lose all of my money when I was just listening to what the other people (who were making millions) were doing?

I kept on journaling my journey on social media venues like LinkedIn and YouTube.

Soon after that, a LinkedIn connection of mine named Guy Spier reached out to me after he saw a video I posted on the platform. He sent me a DM on LinkedIn and said, "Kiana, I know you have a lot of potential, but you're doing this all wrong …"

I was shocked. What did he mean? I was doing what everyone else was doing! And he said something to me that changed my life forever. He said:

CHAPTER THREE

"You've got to stop *trading*, and start *investing* …"

You might be thinking, wait … aren't trading and investing the same thing? Well, the answer is, absolutely not!

I learned from Guy that what I was doing when I lost that $15,000 was trading. I was trying to make a quick profit, which is an incredibly high-risk approach to the online financial markets like stocks, forex, and cryptocurrency.

Here's a quick chart that shows you the differences between trading and investing:

Trading vs. Investing

High risk	Low risk
Short term	Long term
Get rich quick	Build wealth
Requires millions to start	Can start small
All day job	1 hour per week

Trading is very high risk because you're trying to guess whether the market will go up or down day-to-day.

Investing, while there's always risk involved, is typically lower risk because we're choosing investments that will increase in the long term (remember the market value increases 10 to 12%

each year on average).

Trading is done with a short-term goal in mind. Investing is a long-term goal.

Often, when people get into trading, they're hoping for a get rich quick method where they can quit their job and go live on the beach somewhere, which is why they end up making very, very risky trades and losing all of their money.

Investing, on the other hand, is intended to utilize the current surplus of cash that you have and use it to build that into more wealth.

The only people who can actually make money by trading are those who put millions of dollars into the market and are glued to their screen all day.

If you start small when trading, chances are you'll get kicked out of the market just like I did, before you make any money. But when you invest, you can start with a little initial amount without risking too much and slowly grow your portfolio.

Lastly, trading is an all-day job. In order to be an effective day trader, you have to sit in front of the computer, watching charts go up and down from when the market opens at 9:30 a.m. to closing at 4:00 p.m.

But when you're investing, even at the scale that I do it, making $500,000 per year, it only takes about one hour per month, and I'm going to show you exactly how I do that in Chapter 12.

CHAPTER THREE

I took my new friend Guy's advice and I started a new account, this time with $500. I started making my own investments and ignoring all of the hype, trends, click baits, and what other people on Wall Street were telling me to do.

Fast forward three years … I got pregnant with my daughter. So we were going to need more space.

We already had a budget set aside to buy a house, but we then decided that we wanted additional rooms. My husband and I both have family outside the USA and we wanted them to be able to visit and stay with us to babysit and feel comfortable without everyone being in each others' faces. I think it's fair to assume that nobody wants their in-laws to be in their face all the time, right?

This desire required us to stretch ourselves a bit more than we had initially planned. We had $350K set aside for the down payment for our dream house, but our real estate broker showed us this house we absolutely fell in love with. She said if we wanted to make an offer, we needed an additional $50K ASAP.

As we were chatting with her outside of our dream home, I suddenly thought of something. I said, "Let me check out some of my investment accounts."

I pulled up one of my stock brokerage accounts on my iPhone. This was only one of the accounts I'd been managing in the past three years. It was the one I started growing with only $500.

And there it was! In three years, using my Zen Wealth Generator and Invest Diva Diamond Analysis methods, that $500 account had grown to $53K, which means it had grown to 100X the initial investment.

Since I was already in the majority of my investment positions for over a year, we were able to take out the profits without having to pay too much in capital gains tax.

So what did we do?

We took that $500 account—which grew into $50K—and applied it to the down payment on our dream home!

In some cities, this $50K could cover the entire down payment for a house. Do you see what the power of investing can do now?

Can you imagine how much more this account would have compounded if I had started with a bigger initial investment?

Can you see how much money you're leaving on the table by NOT investing your money early?

**The best time to start investing
was 20 years ago.
The second best time is TODAY.**

It took me three years to grow $500 into a house. So let's say you invested $500 today. What would you use it for in three years? What if you continued growing it for five years, or 10?

What if instead of $500, you started with $10K and let it grow into $100K, $500K, or even $1 million over time?

CHAPTER THREE

Would you pay off loans? Turn it into a larger home as I did? Travel the world? Help your family? Think in your head right now, *Five years from now, what would I do with $1 million?*

Not bad for my $1K investment!
Now worth $7,930.84 #divawin.

—Linda H.

Chapter Four

> Money is a
> terrible master
> but an
> excellent servant.
>
> —P.T. Barnum

Learn How to Accelerate Your Portfolio

*I*t was four years into my Invest Diva journey, and I was comfortable with my stock investment strategies for my personal portfolio. My investment accounts were showing consistent returns. I had just gotten hired as an adjunct professor at Baruch College in New York to teach personal finance and investing. On top of that, I was also earning $4K per month as the content creator for an international financial institution.

My goal was to make enough money through my investment account to become financially free. However, my jobs weren't cutting it for a meaningful compounding in my investment accounts.

I was in my mid-thirties and had serious baby fever. But after discussing this with my husband, we realized we couldn't yet afford to bring another person into our family. Plus, if we did have a baby, that would have meant stopping any contributions to my investment account altogether, which would delay our financial freedom journey.

It really sucked that I had to choose between financial security and having a baby. I decided to ask for a promotion from the financial institution I was creating content for. But instead of getting a raise, I got fired. Again. And now I had to find a new job. This continued for a few years. I would get hired by a company, ask for a promotion a few months in, and get fired instead.

After taxes and expenses, I was able to contribute around $500 per month to my investment account. This tiny portfolio slowly but surely grew into $50K in three years. While this is an exceptional return on investment, it barely paid for the downpayment on our dream house, and now I was back to square one, having to rebuild my portfolio from scratch again.

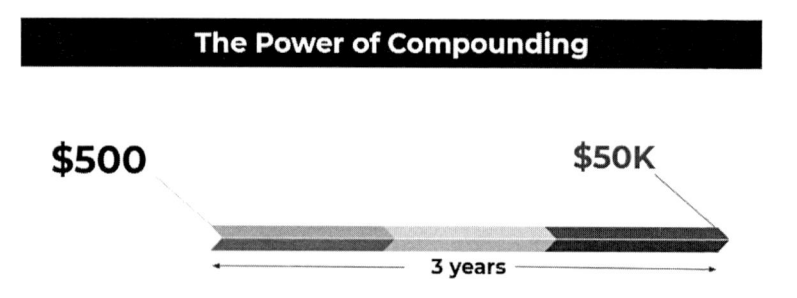

The Power of Compounding

$500 → **$50K**

← 3 years →

What happens when you invest and turn $500 into $50K is called *compounding*. Don't worry about how compounding works right now. We'll go into more detail in Chapter 13.

After seeing this return, I took out my financial calculator to see what would have happened if I had contributed more money into my account monthly. Let's go crazy for a second. What if, instead of just $500 per month, I had contributed $500K per month to my investment account?!

At this rate of return, if I had put in $500K, that investment would have turned into $50 million in those three years!

CHAPTER FOUR

The Power of Compounding

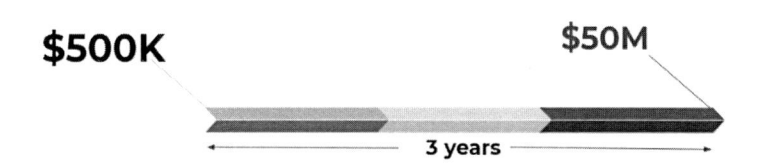

$500K   **$50M**

3 years

In other words, if I continued contributing just $500 per month, even if I continued to show consistently amazing returns on my investment, it would take me over 20 years to achieve financial freedom. It would be way after I'm even able to conceive a baby.

FUN FACT: Did you know that if you invest just $50 per month for your child the moment they're born, they're going to have a million bucks by the time they're 65? Saved and invested, that $40K will turn into $1 million without taking much of your time.

Investing that $50 per month is better than not investing it. A million dollars in 65 years is better than $40K in 65 years.

The best thing you can do with your money if you want to beat inflation and accumulate wealth is to invest it.

However, can you agree that becoming a millionaire in 65 years isn't fast enough?!

I now know that I'm not alone. When I talk to our students who are enrolled in the *Make Your Money Work For You PowerCourse* (learn.investdiva.com) and ask them what is

45

keeping them from reaching a million-dollar portfolio, they typically say it's because they run out of money to invest. They already know *how* to invest ... They're excited about all the new assets and opportunities in the markets ... but they have a ceiling on their income level that's preventing them from contributing to their portfolio.

Investing using low amounts is good, but it's not fast enough!

I knew I needed to find another way to achieve financial freedom.

I needed to start increasing my income so I could accelerate my portfolio's growth.

But I had no clue how to do this. I started modeling all the wealthy people I saw on social media and on TV, trying to find out the secret to their wealth.

I noticed many wealthy people are best-selling authors ... So I wrote the book *Cryptocurrency Investing for Dummies*, published by Wiley, which became a best-seller in its category, but guess who took most of the money that was made through that book? It was split between my agent and my publisher. As a barely known author, I didn't have much negotiation power. Merely getting published by them was their way of doing me a favor.

I was still far away from a Millionaire Diva status or financial freedom.

CHAPTER FOUR

I thought to myself, *If I become famous, I'll become rich.*

So I started to hustle even more. I went on LinkedIn and added every reporter and media producer I could find. I started emailing them relentlessly until they agreed to feature me on their channels.

With the help of a friend and my tenacity, I started getting featured on media like *TIME* magazine, *Forbes*, CNBC, FOX Business, CNN, Yahoo Finance, Cheddar, *Wall Street Journal*, and Insider, to name a few.

But I was still not at a million-dollar portfolio.

I soon realized there was something missing.

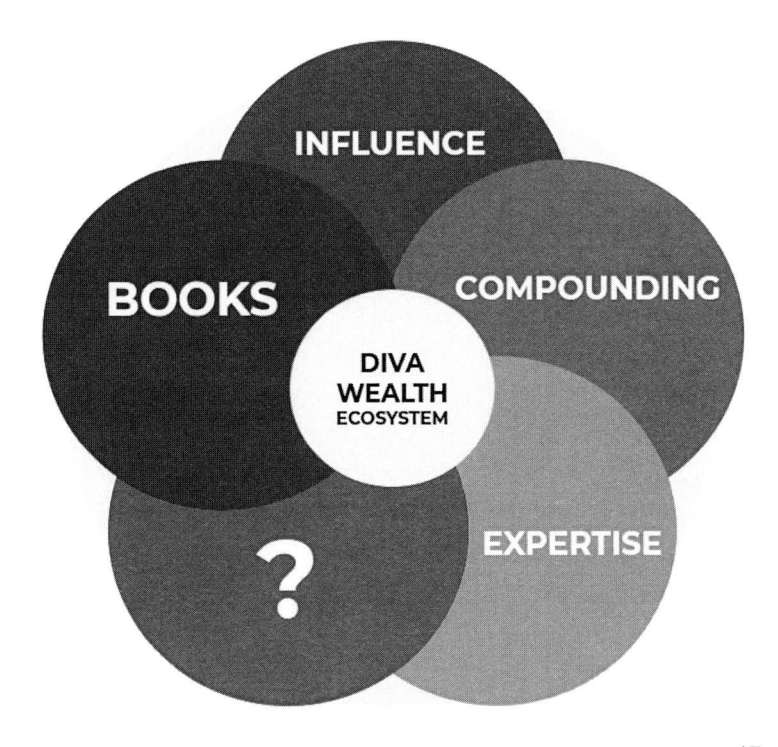

47

Media exposure ALONE wasn't getting me to Millionaire Diva status. Investing with low amounts wasn't getting me to Millionaire Diva status soon *enough*.

So how can we make this happen faster and at a more profound rate? The truth is, these were all parts of what I now call my Diva Wealth Ecosystem.

We all know authors who are broke. Traders who are broke. High-level entrepreneurs who are broke. And celebrities who are broke.

The only people who are able to translate media exposure, hustle, and investing into actual wealth are those who have an ecosystem of products and services that all work together to make a lot of money and a lot of impact.

As one of my favorite authors, Daniel Priestley, puts it:

"It's the ecosystem as a whole that creates the value, NOT any one element of it."

My wealth ecosystem had many elements that could turn me into a Millionaire Diva fast ... but it was missing one very important ingredient. This resulted in years and years of wasted time and left a TON of money on the table.

If I had this ONE key ingredient ten years ago when I first started my Invest Diva journey, I would have probably been on my private island in Bora Bora right now. Which legit makes me angry!

So what was this missing element?

I first heard about this secret ingredient when I was hanging out with my fellow speakers at an investing event in Spain. I was telling my friend, Rob Booker, how frustrated I was with my online business, and how no matter how fancy my website looks and how much media exposure I get, none of it is translating into actual increased income.

He told me, "I know what can solve your problem. What you need to increase your income is to use a *funnel*."

And I'm like, "What's a funnel?"

He went on to tell me how a funnel allows you to streamline your traffic and convert them into paying customers so you can increase your income. That way, you can make more money, invest more money, and compound at an exponential level, so your portfolio grows bigger.

I later learned that a funnel allows you to turn your service, your offer, your practice, your books, your expertise, your influence … into an **automated active income.**

In fact, what my wealth ecosystem was *really* missing was an **offer.**

Myron Golden defines an offer as "An opportunity you give a potential client to exercise their desire to buy (or otherwise obtain) the thing or things that you have helped them realize they've desired all along—at the price that *you* previously decided upon."

You can turn your passion into an offer that creates value for others where they are happy to pay you.

Then, you can turn your offer into an *automated active income* by using a funnel. I'm going to reveal my exact offer and funnel for you later, but here's how things went down …

I always knew I wanted to help more people take control of their financial future. I was passionate about helping women in male-dominated fields. I knew it was especially important for moms to start investing for their children the moment they are born in order to set them up financially.

But I never knew I could turn my passion and expertise into an income-generating offer.

Instead of working a 9–5, building someone else's empire, I could have put the same amount of energy into building my own empire and helping even more people build theirs.

CHAPTER FOUR

DIVA WEALTH ECOSYSTEM

- INFLUENCE
- BOOKS
- COMPOUNDING
- OFFER
- EXPERTISE

Once I learned I could turn my passion into cash that could then be contributed to my investment account, I made a very big decision. I invested in myself to learn about the art of offer creation in a way that creates significant value for others and increases my income in exchange. This single decision completed my Diva Wealth Ecosystem, helping me finally reach the Millionaire Diva status.

From there, my investment account began compounding at an accelerated rate. So much so that in 2021 alone, it went from around $1.5M to just over $5M from January to November, which is the time of the writing of this book.

MILLION DOLLAR FAMILY SECRETS

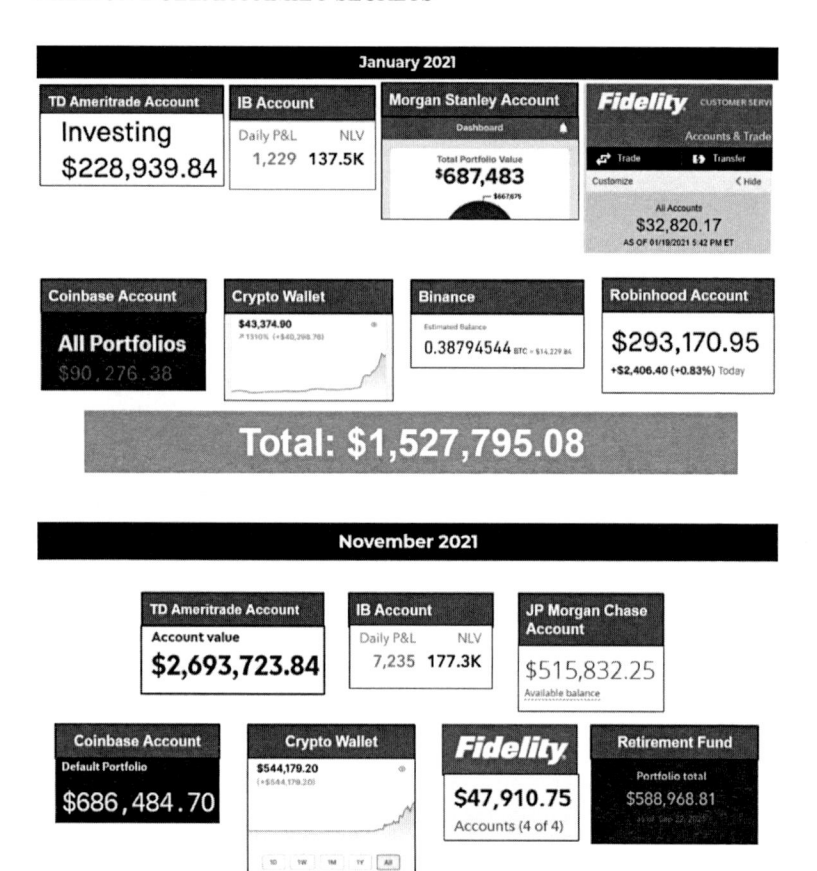

January 2021

TD Ameritrade Account	IB Account	Morgan Stanley Account	Fidelity
Investing $228,939.84	Daily P&L 1,229 / NLV 137.5K	Total Portfolio Value $687,483	All Accounts $32,820.17

Coinbase Account	Crypto Wallet	Binance	Robinhood Account
All Portfolios $90,276.38	$43,374.90	0.38794544 BTC = $14,229.84	$293,170.95 +$2,406.40 (+0.83%) Today

Total: $1,527,795.08

November 2021

TD Ameritrade Account	IB Account	JP Morgan Chase Account
Account value $2,693,723.84	Daily P&L 7,235 / NLV 177.3K	$515,832.25 Available balance

Coinbase Account	Crypto Wallet	Fidelity	Retirement Fund
Default Portfolio $686,484.70	$544,179.20	$47,910.75 Accounts (4 of 4)	Portfolio total $588,968.81

Total: $5,254,399.55

Completing my Diva Wealth Ecosystem has been a blessing, allowing me to work because I want to, not because I have to. I can now sleep with less stress and anxiety around money. I can order food without looking at the price on the menu. I can tip more for services. I can set up a foundation to help support the causes I care about.

Having a Diva Wealth Ecosystem enables us to support the causes that are important to our community. Every year, we take a poll from our students to discover their favorite charities and we contribute to them on behalf of the Invest Diva Movement.

Of course, the money is great. But what is even greater is the profound impact we've been able to make, changing thousands of lives around the world. That's a side effect I didn't foresee.

Thanks to the simple decision I made to create an offer that creates value for others, our students have paid off student debt and mortgages, adopted children, sent their kids to college, paid for health care, started businesses, and even quit their jobs. Some (like my husband and I) are contemplating early retirement, discussing having another baby, or considering moving to their favorite destinations (ours is Hawaii). We're fulfilling our dreams.

Seeing all the results we've been able to create for our students has been far more rewarding than the income alone. Our *Make Your Money Work For You PowerCourse* now has over 3,000 students who share their Diva Wins and Divo Wins on a daily basis.

Reading our student success stories has become a new obsession of mine which keeps me going, even though I no longer even need the money. For example, one of our students, Janee, a burnt-out nurse and a mom of a toddler who joined our Million Dollar Family, was able to accelerate her portfolio to $200K in six short months. And Edyta, a single mom fresh out of an abusive relationship, is now fully in control of not only her finances but also the investment accounts she has set up for her kids.

In the next few chapters, I'll first help you set up your investment portfolio, and then I'll dive deeper into increasing your income and building a Diva Wealth Ecosystem that's going to help you create generational wealth.

In the meantime, if you're serious (not just curious) about increasing your income, visit YourWealthNow.com to secure your spot for our next "Start Building Your Wealth" challenge. I'm not sure if we will run this challenge indefinitely, so please note that there's a chance you won't be able to get in by the time you read this book.

Chapter Five

> Money moves from those who don't put it to work to those who do.
> — Kiana Danial

Create an Account with a Broker/Exchange

You're still here reading this book, so you have probably gotten interested in my story, and maybe even Googled my name to see if I actually know what I am talking about.

By now, you understand that investing is the best thing you can do with your money. But you may be thinking, *Ok, well where do I even start?*

Do I have to go create a bunch of accounts and invest in a bunch of opportunities and hope for them to turn into more money? Should I respond to the DM I just got on Instagram from this person claiming they made a bunch of money with a broker and trying to "hook me up"?

The short answer is no. And please, do not EVER hand your money to someone who slides in your DM without first actually verifying they are legit.

Social media impersonators and fake accounts are the number one reason why people get scammed in the financial industry.

Unfortunately, there is another dark side to today's financial industry, and that is the professional scamming business. If you follow me on any of my social media accounts like Instagram,

Facebook, TikTok, or Twitter, you'll soon start getting messages and followers from someone who looks like me, has a variation of my name or Invest Diva, pretends to be me, and asks you to give them money.

This happens to almost all other legitimate financial institutions and educators. So I'm here to show you how to avoid these by following the right path to making your money work for you.

The first thing you need to do when starting your investing journey is to create an account with a broker or an exchange so that you can get access to the online financial markets.

What Is a Broker?

It's never been easier to invest in online financial assets thanks to the advent of the Internet and online brokers. An online brokerage allows you to access the financial markets and participate in the buying and selling of financial instruments like stocks. Online brokers are the intermediary between buyers and sellers. They facilitate the purchase and sale of financial assets in an online environment and typically make money by charging the investors a commission fee or by adding a markup to the stock price.

There are online brokers in almost all countries. Regardless of where you are, you should be able to invest, but make sure that you're selecting a credible broker.

Depending on the asset type you're planning to invest in (i.e., stocks, cryptocurrency, or forex) you may need to find a specialized broker or exchange.

Choosing a Stock Brokerage

Choosing a broker, just like anything else in personal finance, is personal. You need to find a broker that suits your needs. At Invest Diva, we encourage investors to participate in "Value Investing" as I explained in Chapter 3. This means buying an asset and holding it long-term to maximize gains. In that case, you wouldn't need the highly advanced brokerage accounts that are mainly used by large hedge funds and day traders, which can also save you a ton of money on commission fees.

As more people become interested in investing on their own, many online brokers have adopted the passive investing style, and many even forgo the commission fee charged on your transactions because you are parking your money in their brokerage long term.

The most important things to remember before choosing a broker are the level of regulation, trust, and insurance. Here's the checklist of things to look for in the terms or disclaimer portion of their website. You can also look up the brokerage on the SIPC website.

1. Your brokerage must be a member of the Financial Industry Regulatory Authority (FINRA).

2. Your brokerage must be covered by the Federal Deposit Insurance Corporation (FDIC).

3. Your brokerage must carry insurance with a per-customer limit of at least $500,000, with $250,000 available for cash claims. If you're looking to invest more than this amount, then you need to either diversify among several brokers or call your broker and ask for increased insurance.

4. Your brokerage should also be willing to reimburse you for losses resulting from fraud. Make sure you double-check what the brokerage requires of you in order for you to be reimbursed. Find out if you have to provide any documentation or take specific precautions to protect yourself.

Here are some brokerages for stocks in the US, UK, European Union, Australia, and Canada that either myself or our Invest Diva students have used with an acceptable level of satisfaction:

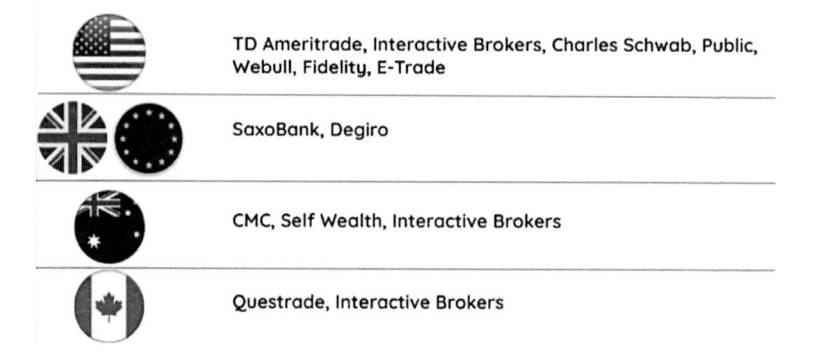

🇺🇸	TD Ameritrade, Interactive Brokers, Charles Schwab, Public, Webull, Fidelity, E-Trade
🇬🇧 🇪🇺	SaxoBank, Degiro
🇦🇺	CMC, Self Wealth, Interactive Brokers
🇨🇦	Questrade, Interactive Brokers

Almost all of the above brokerages facilitate investing in all international and US stocks, as well as Index Funds. If you're looking to diversify outside of the stock market and into assets such as cryptocurrency, then you need to find a specialized exchange or broker that can facilitate cryptocurrency investments.

Choosing a Cryptocurrency Exchange

The most popular way to buy cryptocurrencies is to go directly through an online cryptocurrency exchange. However, depending on your cryptocurrency investing goals, you may need to consider alternative methods. For example, if you're an active crypto trader, you may find a traditional cryptocurrency exchange or a broker easier to use. But if you just want to buy some cryptos and park them in your wallet, a trusted online/local exchange can do the job. In this chapter, I tell you all about different types of exchanges, brokers, and other cryptocurrency providers and show you how to choose the right one(s) for your cryptocurrency goals.

The most popular type of cryptocurrency exchange is called *Centralized Exchanges.* Centralized exchanges are like traditional stock exchanges. The buyers and sellers come together, and the exchange plays the role of a middleman. These exchanges typically charge a commission to facilitate the transactions made between buyers and sellers.

Here's how a centralized exchange typically works:

1. You give your money to the exchange.

2. The exchange holds it for you (like a bank or a trusted middleman).

3. You watch the prices of the available cryptocurrencies on the exchange.

4. Depending on the exchange, you can trade your fiat currency (a traditional currency, like the US dollar) for a cryptocurrency (like Bitcoin). With most exchanges, however, you will find better luck exchanging two cryptocurrencies for one another.

5. You place your order.

6. The exchange finds a seller to match your buy order. If you're selling, the exchange finds you a buyer.

7. Tada! You just crypto shopped on an exchange.

In my book, *Cryptocurrency Investing for Dummies* (published by Wiley, 2019), I go into further detail about choosing crypto exchanges and the best investing practices that are beyond the scope of this book.

Some of my favorite cryptocurrency exchanges in the US include Coinbase, Gemini, and Kraken.

Recently, stockbrokers such as Robinhood have also enabled cryptocurrency trading features, but there's a big catch. One of the biggest reasons people invest in cryptocurrency is to buy and hold long-term to maximize capital gains. Please note that if you invest in cryptocurrencies through a broker such as Robinhood, you will not actually own the cryptocurrency. You will simply be taking a position on its price.

Please promise me that you won't invest in cryptocurrency before actually understanding how it works. To find out if it suits your risk tolerance, go through the *Seven Deadly Mistakes Crypto Investors Make (And How to Avoid Them)* on **www.CryptoMistakes.com**.

Pro Tip: Once you choose your broker, always make sure you activate the Two-Factor Authentication (2FA) on your platform. Two-factor authentication is a method of confirming your claimed identity by using a combination of two different factors: something the exchange knows (like your password) and something it has (like a six-digit number it sends to your mobile phone or your email address for the second step of the verification).

I opened my account and made a small investment before I found this class but was scared. Now I feel empowered and today my money is up $5,000. I'm on my way to $100,000 Diva then Million Dollar Diva!! Thank you. #divawin

—Kimberly A.

Chapter Six

> Financial literacy isn't a side effect of wealth ... Wealth is a side effect of financial literacy.
>
> —Kiana Danial

Figure Out Where You Stand Financially

I was born into a Jewish family and raised in Iran in the midst of a Middle Eastern war. My dad, who previously was a very successful engineer and CEO of a construction company, had just lost everything to the new Iranian regime. The government took over all my dad's assets and froze his bank account. They were actually going to kill him, but he somehow lucked out, and he didn't get executed. But still, they took all his money and banned him from leaving the country, so I grew up with almost nothing.

When I turned 18 years old, I went to study in Japan by myself. While my time in Japan was pretty tough, one of the key ingredients of my investing system that allows me to beat the boys of Wall Street is thanks to a Japanese investing method I learned when I went back to Japan to work with Japanese hedge funds. This is something they use to beat the boys of Wall Street at their own game!

I will teach you about how that Japanese method works in Chapter 11. But don't fast forward before completing this step because NOT taking this step is the EXACT reason why 96% of traders lose money in the markets.

Throughout my journey from Iran to Japan to New York, I went through many ups and downs. And my financial situation, and more importantly, **risk tolerance**, fluctuated with it.

Your risk tolerance is the combination of your willingness and your ability to take a risk.

When my dad was at the top of his game at a young age, his willingness and ability to take a risk were high. If cryptocurrency had existed back then, he probably would have exposed his portfolio to it. That way, because of the decentralized nature of cryptocurrencies like Bitcoin, when the Iranian government invaded our house to take all his assets, he still would have been able to support my mom and two older siblings.

When I was single and freelancing in New York, my willingness to take a risk was higher, but my ability to take a risk was lower because I wasn't making that much money. So the better option for me would have been to invest a small amount (like $50/ month) in a low-risk Index Fund like VOO.

Years later, after I gave birth to my daughter, my brain was on snooze and my willingness to take a risk went down. But my husband got a bonus, so our ability to take a risk went higher. I adjusted my system, so when I was on maternity leave, my system was making me on average $9,580 per month.

Your risk tolerance also depends on your life cycle.

For example, between the ages of 25–45, you're probably more growth-oriented. Between the ages of 45–60, you're conservation/protection-oriented. After 60, it's probably going to be your retirement years, and you're concerned about generating income, protecting what you have, or maybe about gifting to your grandchildren and family members and creating generational wealth, which is our ultimate goal with our *Million Dollar Family Accelerator*.

The more detailed you get with your risk tolerance, the more successful you'll be with your investment strategy because you'll be able to make confident decisions. People who don't invest according to their risk tolerance are more likely to fall for the hype and FOMO the media constantly creates.

> **Use Invest Diva's risk management tool kit to identify your ABILITY and WILLINGNESS to take a risk by attending the free masterclass at:**
>
> **learn.investdiva.com**

In the risk management tool kit that I'll send to your email after you complete the training, you can calculate your exact risk tolerance on your own, without doing any math. Just pick up your smartphone and punch in some numbers.

Kiana is a smart and amazing coach. She has a great and very helpful team and coaches. I have a degree in Finance and I have to say that what I learned in 8 weeks with Kiana is way more than what I learned from going to one of the top business schools in the USA!

—Rawan A.

Chapter Seven

> Working because you want to,
> not because you have to,
> is financial freedom.
>
> — *Tony Robbins*

Clarify Your Financial Goals

When we run our Invest Diva 5-Day Challenge, I spend a whole day teaching about financial goal setting. Some of our attendees ask me, "Kiana, why do you have to spend one whole day of the challenge setting goals? I just want a bunch of money! How hard is that?"

Here's why:

You need to set financial goals so you can create a strategy to actually achieve them.

Napoleon Hill said, "A goal is a dream with a deadline." I want to one-up Napoleon Hill and say:

A goal is a measurable dream that feels achievable to you, with a deadline.

You can't start investing by just saying, "Well, I just want to make a bunch of money! The more the better!"

You need to have a specific plan with a feasible deadline that feels achievable to you. Once you get to your first goal, then you can move on to the next level just like I did. I went from a $50K goal to a $100K goal, to $200K, to a $1 million goal. Now that I have the system going for me, my portfolio is on track to grow to $100 million in the next five years.

You want the deadline to be specific and achievable to you as well, so you can actually believe to your core that you can make it happen. This forces you to then go and find the resources to make your goal happen fast.

Think to yourself, *Why am I investing?* The answer normally falls into one or more of the following options:

- Income
- Retirement
- Generational wealth

You need to write down exactly why you're investing. This will help you pick the right assets for your unique goals and financial situation as well as invest in the exact right time frame.

For example, when I first got started investing, I had just been fired from my job and I needed to pay rent, so I was investing to make an income, which was clearly more high risk and didn't work out very well for me, as I explained in Chapter 3.

But now I have other streams of income, so the majority of my investments are to make my money work for me on the side, to grow my wealth for my retirement years, and to create generational wealth for my daughter and future children.

In my opinion, generational wealth is the best reason to start investing. It has become the core of our education at Invest Diva. We achieve investing for generational wealth through a simple framework I created called the Zen Wealth Generator.

zenwealthgenerator.com

I talk more about the Zen Wealth Generator in Chapter 13.

CHAPTER SEVEN

But for now, here's a glimpse of how the Zen Wealth Generator works:

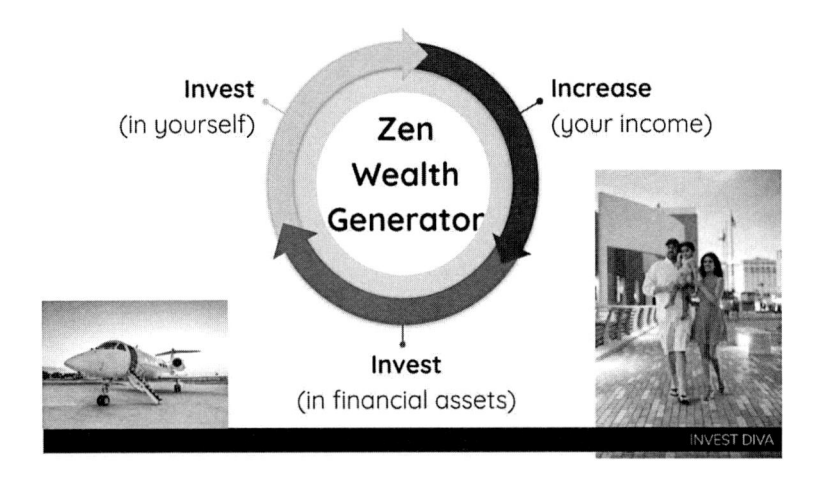

Diagram: Zen Wealth Generator cycle — Invest (in yourself) → Increase (your income) → Invest (in financial assets)

Step 1: INVEST (in yourself)

Every time I set a new financial goal for myself, I start with investing in myself, which means I spend time and money to learn new skills that add value to my life and increase my income.

For example, you are investing your time right now to learn this new skill by reading this book.

Step 2: INCREASE (your income)

I have streams of income other than investing, and I continue to add to them. Some examples include the royalties from my books, earnings from creating financial content for my corporate clients like Nasdaq, dividend payments from select stocks, and affiliate partnerships with my network that I've been growing over the years. On top of these, I also have my Invest Diva business, which helps me lower my taxes.

Step 3: INVEST (in financial assets)

The third phase of my Zen Wealth Generator is contributing a portion of my cash flow to my investment portfolio on a monthly basis. I continually invest in financial assets to make my money work for me.

In other words, I keep on compounding my investments in myself, which helps me compound my income, which helps me compound my investments.

This is exactly how I make more money, my money makes me money, and the money my money makes also makes more money without much additional effort on my end.

You cannot achieve true financial freedom and generational wealth unless all three of these elements are working in tandem.

Now that you have an understanding of how creating generational wealth works, let's get back to setting your financial goals.

The Three Rules of Financial Goal-Setting:

1) Measurable

2) Realistic

3) Has a Deadline

I sometimes ask my friends, "What's your goal in life?"

And they'll say, "I wanna be happy!"

I mean, that's great! You can and should be happy. But that doesn't need an investment strategy. You can be super happy right this minute. That's just a decision and a shift of mindset that needs to be made.

Every time I get together with our Million Dollar Family Accelerator or Inner Circle members, we spend a few moments celebrating our wins and feeling the happiness that's driven by our gratitude. You can, in fact, close your eyes, think of three things that you are grateful for, and feel incredibly joyful—right this second.

With this, we've established that you don't need a financial goal to feel happy. But you need one to reach the measurable numbers you set for yourself. So, when you're setting your goals, you want them to be measurable.

Here are some examples:

- $700,000 net worth
- $3.5 million house in Westport, Connecticut
- 250% return on investment
- $40,000 college education fund
- $1 million retirement account
- $50,000 charitable amount
- Leaving a $50 million legacy
- Helping 1 million moms take control of their financial future (Hint: This is one of my five-year goals)

Now, I just threw out these numbers, but before you just go ahead and set random goals, remember that …

Your goals need to BE and FEEL realistic to YOU.

If your goals feel unachievable to you, you likely will get overwhelmed and quit by week two.

Yes, your goals should be challenging and outside of your comfort zone, but no, they should not be ridiculous or unattainable. Setting a goal to save $1,000,000 when saving $10,000 is already a stretch just leaves you feeling defeated. Start with a goal that is within reach. For example, if saving $5,000 a year is easy for you, then why not make your goal $10,000?

The good news is, once you make your first micro-achievement, then you can set higher goals as you win.

I made the mistake of setting unrealistic goals in the past. When I first got into this 10 years ago, I kept telling myself that I wanted to make $7 million. I kept repeating it, and I thought the law of attraction was just going to make it happen.

But it didn't. I got my first major success when I made my goal achievable to ME.

In 2019, I joined Russell Brunson's VIP group, which was called the "Two Comma Club"—it's called the Two Comma Club because there are two commas in the number 1,000,000.

Once I joined, I kept seeing all these members, people who were my peers in the same program, getting their Two Comma Club Awards. Seeing them achieving that micro-goal made it more believable to me.

That's when I changed my goal from $7 million to $1 million, and BAM! I literally made not only $1 million in my business, but also $1 million in my investments within a year.

Once I achieved that goal, I started moving up the ladder and set up my next goal at $10 million because it finally felt achievable to me.

Now, here I'd also add a sub-rule, and that is, **surround yourself with people who have already achieved the goals you want to achieve**, because seeing them reach their goals is going to make it that much more believable for you.

This is the reason why I encourage our *Make Your Money Work For You PowerCourse* and *Million Dollar Family Accelerator* members to announce their DivaWins, big or small, as they go through our programs.

No matter how small their win is, it might encourage someone else in the group who's still not there, and we've been seeing an amazing shift in our group's energy ever since we saw multiple people reaching $100K and $1 million profit in their investment accounts.

Let's get to the final rule in goal setting:

It MUST have a deadline.

Again, back in the day, when I was a Welfare Diva (not a Millionaire Diva), I kept saying I want to make $7 million, but I didn't specify in what amount of time—in five years, 10 years, 50 years?

Rest assured, I will reach that $7 million (I may have reached it by the time you're reading this book!), but I didn't get there during the first ten years of my investing journey. Why? Because my goal didn't have a deadline.

I learned this principle from Jack Canfield, the co-creator of the *Chicken Soup for the Soul* series and co-author of *The Success*

Principles. I interviewed him for one of our YouTube episodes about goal-setting a few years ago, and I was explaining to him how I hadn't yet achieved some of my goals, no matter how hard I tried.

He said, "Kiana, set a deadline. The more detailed the better. And when you're writing it down, write it in the present tense as if today is the day that you achieved your goal."

This literally changed my life. Now on my vision board, I have all these micro-achievements that are measurable, realistic to me, and have a deadline. As I reach those goals, I move them to the "completed" side of my board and start setting new goals using the exact method I shared with you here.

I'd love to hear your goals! If you feel like sharing them publicly so you have an accountability partner, snap a photo of this book with your phone, upload it to your Instagram Stories, declare your measurable, realistic goals with your deadline. Be sure to tag @InvestDiva so I can cheer you on!

My husband and I just bought our new home thanks to you. Just by finishing the first few modules, we've been able to increase our wealth by over 37 percent. Thank you so much and God bless you and your family Kiana.

—Nicole S.

Chapter Eight

> The challenge is not
> to pick the best investment.
> The challenge is to pick
> the right investment.
>
> — *Don Connelly*

Go Asset Picking

*N*ow that you have a broker, know where you stand financially, and have set measurable, realistic goals with a deadline, it's time to pick the right assets that suit you and nobody else!

It's true when they say …

Personal finance is personal.

I get DMs and comments on social media from my followers on a daily basis, saying:

"Kiana! Just tell me ONE stock to buy that's going to make me a millionaire!"

To which my response is: "It doesn't work that way!"

We are different people in different financial situations, with different risk tolerances, and different financial goals. My understanding of certain companies and my level of confidence in them is different from yours because of the unique experiences and interactions I've had with them.

There are several paths to generational wealth when it comes to investing. The ones that are guaranteed to get you to your destination are those you have the highest level of confidence in.

Notice I said *you*. Not me. If I tell you Bitcoin is great, but you don't even know what gives Bitcoin its value, you're going to fall for all the hype and FOMO the media is throwing your way, and you're guaranteed to lose all your money in no time.

That's why one of the easiest ways to start investing is by simply going through your credit card statement and seeing which companies you spend the most amount of money with on a monthly basis.

Look for companies you like so much that you would dread switching to their competitors. If they're public companies, this could give you the basics for your investment strategy development.

Generally, when it comes to asset picking, I do things differently. Instead of "looking at the company's short-term financials," and going through thousands of their previous quarter's financial reports, I look for:

- Category kings
- Companies that improve life
- Companies that solve problems
- Companies that allow us to do things better, faster, and cheaper
- And most important of all, companies that do something good for humankind

Published growth trends, profit margins, and price-to-earnings (P/E) ratios are not as important as understanding how a company could create value in the years ahead.

So as millionaire Divas (and Divos), we don't blindly buy a stock we heard about from our brother-in-law and hold on to it. As millionaire Divas (and Divos), we buy the right ones and hold on to them as a method of value investing. We're not stuck to our screens all day, engaging in unproductive activity.

Now let's go one level deeper. I'm going to reveal the best way to go asset picking so that you don't fall for all the hype and FOMO created by little birdies. This is actually the Warren Buffett-approved method of asset picking. It's super powerful, and it's something I'd recommend that you remind yourself over and over again.

> **"When picking an asset, look at it as if you're going to buy the whole company."**
> **—Warren Buffett**

Kiana Danial takes it one level deeper. I say, when picking an asset, look at it as if you're going to find the one to get married to and stick with through sickness and in health.

Imagine you have $3 trillion ready to purchase your next big company and become its CEO. Out of all the thousands of companies out there … big or small, those who are already established, and those who are just getting started, you can only choose ONE. The one and only perfect match you're going to commit to and "marry."

Will you buy Apple? Will you buy Whole Foods? Will you buy Pfizer? Will you buy Facebook, Uber, Disney? Remember, you're buying the whole company.

In Chapter 11, I show you why it's actually good to plan for a divorce when it comes to asset picking and how you can even be in multiple committed relationships with different assets in your portfolio!

Monogamy is not a good thing when it comes to investing and creating multiple revenue streams.

This just got weird. But for now, at this point, you need to spend all your energy in finding the best asset you could possibly find to marry. You can either go with a company you actually know and use or go to websites like Yahoo! Finance, StockCard.io, and Morning Star for inspiration.

Happy Asset Picking!

Chapter Nine

> Money is only a tool.
> It will take you wherever
> you wish, but it will not
> replace you as a driver.

— *Ayn Rand*

Create a Unique Investment Strategy Based on Your Risk Tolerance and Financial Goals

Can you set $500 aside every month?

How about $250? $100? If you're anything like the old me, when I had a Welfare Diva mindset, I'm guessing you spend way too much on things that don't add real value to your life. I used to buy things I knew were going to get lost in the back of my closet and never get worn. But I simply purchased them to gain instant gratification.

There are so many things we buy on a daily basis that aren't necessary, like all the stuff you have in your house that you never use—cable, things you buy to impress others, or things to keep up with your neighbors—that are not actual assets or investments.

I'm not saying those are bad. In fact, one of the benefits of financial freedom and achieving the Millionaire Diva status is that I no longer even look at price tags when I purchase things.

But in order to get to that level, you first need to take the steps necessary to make sure you are consistently investing in your portfolio and making your money work for you. It's the squeeze period.

For an apple seed to turn into an apple tree, it first needs to go under the ground. So does your initial investment before you achieve financial freedom.

The good news is, once you receive my risk management tool kit in your inbox after attending my free masterclass at **learn.investdiva.com**, you're going to find out EXACTLY how much money you should be investing!

Some of our students actually get shocked after filling out the tool kit, because they find out they had a higher risk tolerance than they thought they had. This is because your ability and willingness to take a risk are two different factors, but most people can't recognize the difference simply by looking at their bank account or by trying to feel how high their risk tolerance is.

For example, one of my students, Cynthia, who is a social media manager and a single mom to an 18-year-old, was surprised to find out that her risk tolerance was medium to high. She had no experience with investing or anything financially-related. She got into our *Make Your Money Work For You PowerCourse*, started her Invest Diva journey, and made her first profit in only two months.

Now she continues to grow her money, which has enabled her to fulfill her dream of buying a van house (RV) and traveling around the country while sipping mimosas.

One of our other students, Grace from Australia, joined our

PowerCourse a year before the pandemic. She works in healthcare and at the time had higher risk tolerance, so she started investing in a few assets, but then got busy with work and forgot all about her investment portfolio.

Once the pandemic hit, all of Australia went into total lockdown, so she lost her job.

She then remembered her portfolio she had created a year ago thanks to her Invest Diva journey, and to her surprise, it had grown by over 100%. Some of the best-performing assets in her portfolio that she had picked from our Premium Investing Group (PIG) analysis had grown over 200% in a year.

She then joined our *Million Dollar Family Accelerator* program to work on her goal of achieving her Millionaire Diva status.

On the other hand, we had a different student, Edyta, who was disappointed to find out her risk tolerance was lower than what she had thought.

She focused on budgeting and increasing her income so she could consistently contribute $100 to her portfolio, investing in lower-risk assets. She slowly grew her account and kept compounding both her income and investments until she achieved her $100K Diva status.

The reason I'm telling you these stories is to emphasize the importance of investing based on your risk tolerance, and creating an investment strategy that suits your situation. There are multiple paths to wealth, and your goal is to find the right journey for you, so you don't keep panicking or get demotivated along the way.

I put together the whole process in a five-step framework I call the Invest Diva Diamond Analysis (IDDA). Just like a diamond, it has five points.

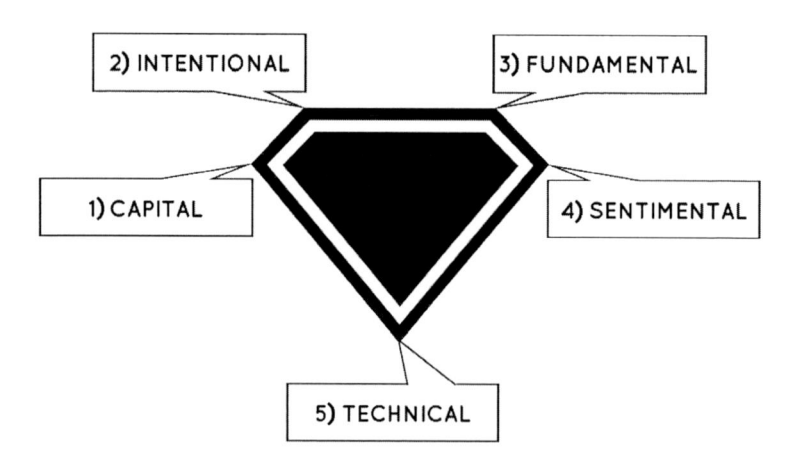

```
        2) INTENTIONAL          3) FUNDAMENTAL

  1) CAPITAL                          4) SENTIMENTAL

              5) TECHNICAL
```

So far we've discussed the first three points:

1) Capital: Understanding where you stand financially.
2) Intentional: Setting your financial goals.
3) Fundamental: Picking the right asset for your portfolio based on your *Capital* and *Intentional* analysis.

In the next chapters, I cover points 4 and 5, Sentimental and Technical analysis, respectively.

Chapter Ten

> All the math you need in the stock market you get in the fourth grade.
>
> —*Peter Lynch*

Follow the "No-Math" Investing Method

One of the biggest questions I get asked from people who are interested in creating generational wealth by making their money work for them is, "Kiana, this is such a cool idea. But I'm not a math whiz. I literally get a headache when I look at numbers. Can I still do this?"

Even though all these Wall Street hedge fund managers spend years studying pure math, I've always suspected that there's no math needed when investing.

Personally, I suck at math. Yes, I'm aware that I studied electrical engineering, but those were some of the most exasperating years of my life, and I barely graduated. Ever since I started investing based on my Invest Diva Diamond Analysis Method, I never use any math, and I am growing my account.

But to be honest, I was still curious to see if I was an exception.

In this chapter, I'm going to show you exactly why you do not need any math to invest successfully on your own. The most math you'll ever need when investing is equivalent to what you learned in second grade. Even for that, you can use your calculator on your phone.

In fact, throughout my research, I found out that sometimes…

Being a math wiz can actually cost you when it comes to investing.

But before I get there, let me tell you the story of one of our Invest Diva students, who is a brain tumor survivor. She underwent a very complicated surgery to remove the tumor. Thankfully, the tumor was removed successfully, so she got her health back.

However, as a result of the surgery, she lost the ability to speak, write, and count. She had to relearn how to do the simplest of tasks. Her IQ verifiably dropped to the level of a child. While she has since relearned how to speak and write, she still to this day can't do anything more than second-grade math.

After hearing me talk about the No-Math Investing Method, she decided to join the Invest Diva movement to push herself, test her limits, and perhaps even to prove me wrong!

The result? After finishing our eight-week PowerCourse, she not only learned the process but she also started a small retirement fund suitable to her low-medium risk tolerance and beat the market average in her second year.

This has been one of the most inspiring stories within our Invest Diva community.

The truth is, even Wall Street hedge fund managers know the markets aren't about complicated math equations.

I was chatting with a highly successful Wall Street investment banker the other day, and he admitted that his years of studying pure math at Harvard and MIT play no role in his investment decisions.

When digging even deeper, I found out math geniuses actually sometimes mismanage the emotional aspect of investing so much that they underperform compared with their peers! To make matters even worse, these math geniuses have the delusion that they know more than others. This is detrimental when it comes to managing your portfolio.

The majority of ego-driven math geniuses thrive on being right. So when they win, they get super excited and announce it to the world. Unfortunately, the moment their portfolio starts heading down—something that is very normal in the stock market, by the way—they feel the need to find a quick "math" solution to make up for the losses.

Oftentimes, they end up digging a deeper hole and turn their portfolio into a Las Vegas casino just to prove to the world that they are right and "smart."

Here's the real secret to the financial markets:

The markets aren't about math but about psychology.

More specifically, the markets are about finding out what other traders and investors are feeling ... and managing your emotions.

The majority of the crowd tries to solve a short-term problem, but instead creates a long-term disaster.

You can especially see the negative impacts of crowd psychology during market crashes and times of economic downturn. When emotions are high, novice investors will try to solve a short-term problem by panic-selling their assets. But short-sightedness leads to depriving their families of generational wealth.

This led me to another fascinating discovery. Thanks to naturally higher emotional intelligence:

Research shows that women are BETTER at investing than men.

Female investors outperform their male counterparts because they have a longer-term outlook and aren't investing to "win" a game—they're investing for long-term financial security, oftentimes to protect themselves and their offspring.

I'm sharing this statistic not to undermine our Invest Divos, but to empower our Invest Divas. The good news is, emotional intelligence is a skill that can be acquired through training. So if you're like me, and weren't born with naturally high emotional intelligence, then you're in luck, because this is something that you can acquire through practicing the right habits!

Chapter Eleven

> Be greedy
> when others are fearful.
> Be fearful
> when others are greedy.
>
> — *Warren Buffett*

Learn the Art of Buying Low and Selling High

The first time I ever sold something for a profit was back when I was in Japan and went for a quick visit back to Iran.

One of the biggest perks of living in Japan is that you're consistently exposed to the highest-end electronics and gadgets at a really low and competitive price. Sometimes it becomes problematic though, as you can easily get addicted to constantly upgrading to the next model of your gadgets.

For me, this addiction showed itself in the form of purchasing cameras because I love taking pictures.

If you were born any time before the year 2008, you might remember that back in the day, our phones didn't have cameras. Even if they did, they were nowhere as high quality as an actual digital camera.

Being a fan of photography, I found myself purchasing the newer models of digital cameras year after year to get a better pixel and a higher quality.

I kept my old cameras in a box in my closet. One summer break, as I was planning to go back to Iran to visit my family, I decided to bring the old cameras with me to see if I could give them to anyone who might be interested.

I wasn't even planning on selling them! *Who in their right mind would want an old model of a camera?* I thought.

As it turned out, due to sanctions, people in Iran were not able to get the latest gadgets in many categories. So when I opened my mouth to talk about my "old" digital cameras, I had friends lining up, begging to pay me for them. Initially, I purchased the cameras using the Japanese yen. When I sold them, even though I sold them for less than what I had paid for them, thanks to the favorable exchange rate (and after the conversions and the fluctuations of the foreign exchange market), I ended up making money!

This was my first ever return on investment, which also taught me a valuable lesson about the foreign exchange (forex) market, something that came in handy when I started trading forex years later.

But at the end of the day, the name of the game of profit-making is this:

Buy low and sell high.

You see this phenomenon in business. In e-commerce. In real estate. And even when investing in yourself.

For example, when I pay my coach $100K to learn how to sell high-ticket items (buy low) so that I can make $1 million in a day (sell high), it means I invested in myself at a lower price ($100K) compared to the expected rate of return ($1 million).

When I invested $2,000 in myself to learn how to read off the teleprompter (buy low), which led me to get a freelancing reporter gig at the NYSE which paid me $4,000 per month (sell high), I again followed this principle.

Literally, everyone in the marketplace wants to do this exact thing. Not just you, not just me, but even the big boys of Wall Street.

The good news is, the art of buying low and selling high has a super cool rhythm to it when it comes to the online financial markets. And this is exactly where we can go to beat the boys of Wall Street at their own game (and we've done it over and over again in the past decade) using a really cool Japanese method and an even cooler Italian method.

These are my go-to weapons when it comes to analyzing the markets because they not only help me figure out what the rest of the market is looking at, but they also help me stay ahead of them.

I learned about this when I was doing a freelance consulting gig for a backend Wall Street company that did frequency trading. They wanted to expand their services in Japan, so they hired me to teach them about the Japanese business culture so they could win with their potential customers. I ended up traveling back to Japan with them a bunch of times, and at one of our corporate after parties with one of the Japanese clients, I ended up talking in-depth about market sentiment and technical analysis.

There was a guy called Sato-san who told me about a Japanese financial indicator that helps their company in Japan figure out what the Wall Street firms are doing, so they can go in and beat them at their own game.

What's even more awesome is that I later learned we can tune the system so it correlates to our risk tolerance. So the whole Invest Diva Diamond Analysis came back full circle for me.

Introducing: Ichimoku

As I showed you in Chapter 6, you first need to find out if your risk tolerance is low, medium, or high, or something in between these three big categories.

Your Unique Risk Tolerance ...

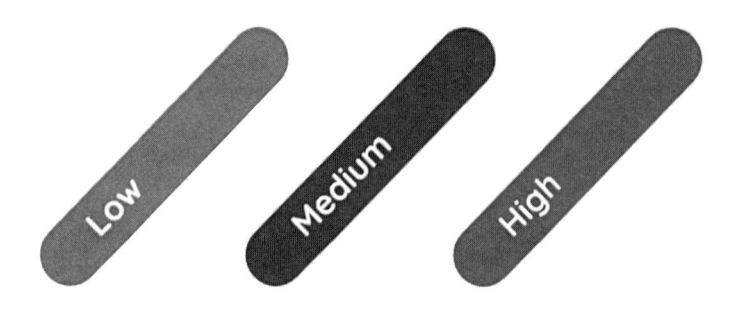

Low Medium High

Once you know your EXACT unique risk tolerance, you can plug it into my system to make great investments that are just perfect for you and no one else, and you get to compound your money so it works for you on your behalf while you're out there enjoying your life.

This system is kind of like the ski slopes. If you follow me on social media, you probably know that I'm actually a double-black-diamond skier.

But when I'm teaching my three-year-old daughter how to ski, I'm first going to take her on the bunny slopes. If you're a beginner skier, you should only go down the green. As you get more advanced, you can make your way to the black diamond.

My system works the same way ...

If you have a high-risk tolerance, then choose a high-risk asset, and use the first Ichimoku signal.

If you have a medium-risk tolerance, then choose a medium-risk asset, and use the second Ichimoku signal.

As your risk tolerance goes low, you have to wait for the third Ichimoku signal to get in a trade.

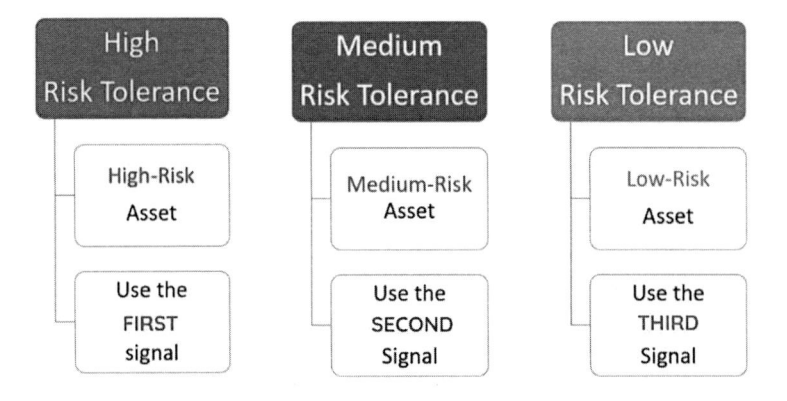

High Risk Tolerance	Medium Risk Tolerance	Low Risk Tolerance
High-Risk Asset	Medium-Risk Asset	Low-Risk Asset
Use the FIRST signal	Use the SECOND Signal	Use the THIRD Signal

It's as simple as 1, 2, 3. Can you count to 3? Then you know enough math to use my system.

The Chipotle Experiment

One of my favorite fast-food restaurants has always been Chipotle Mexican Grill. Back in 2017, they closed down all their restaurants because they made people sick with a foodborne outbreak. Its stock price crashed like there was no tomorrow because the market sentiment was very negative. The whole media trashed its stock and created a panic for Chipotle investors, which resulted in the majority of shareholders selling their Chipotle stocks.

Meanwhile, my system showed me that Chipotle was fast becoming UNDERVALUED and if I have a medium risk tolerance, I should actually buy Chipotle once its price bottoms out at a key psychological level. But how much can I wait before I buy? I want to buy at the cheapest price when stuff is on sale.

By using the technical point of the Invest Diva Diamond system, I found out it could go to as low as $270 if I was willing to risk not buying at all if it doesn't drop that low, which matched my risk tolerance perfectly.

Someone who had a higher risk tolerance than me could have bought their way down to $270 so they didn't risk missing out.

CHAPTER ELEVEN

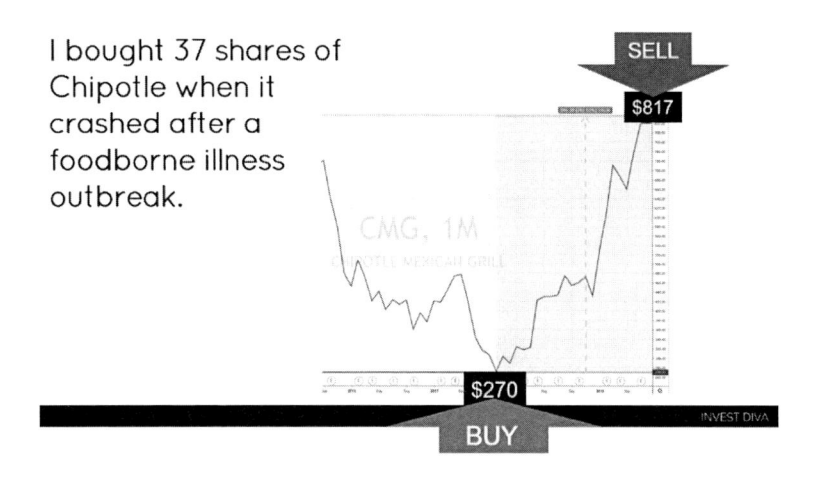

> I bought 37 shares of Chipotle when it crashed after a foodborne illness outbreak.
>
> SELL $817
> BUY $270
> CMG, 1M

For me, $270 worked, and I bought 37 Chipotle shares when it dropped to the bottom. Only 15 months later, the stock price was above and beyond where it was BEFORE the crash. This means it gave me a 202% return on investment, which means I made $30,200 pure profit in just over one year without doing ANY math!

So now I get to eat Chipotle every day with the profits I made.

Jokes aside, this goes to show that I no longer need money managers to invest on my behalf. I don't use any math when analyzing the market sentiment, and I can access my profit anytime I want. This way I don't have to lock my money away in the hedge fund of some account manager who is likely going to underperform the market and sell based on market fear, as well as penalizing me if I ever need to get my money out!

Since the inception of the Invest Diva Movement, our students have been compounding their money on their own, without having to rely on others. Our students have ranged from high school graduates to stay-at-home moms, entrepreneurs, professionals, and even rocket scientists who weren't able to make their money work for them prior to joining the Invest Diva Movement. You can do this too!

Chapter Twelve

> If your money isn't
> having babies,
> you're preventing yourself
> from creating
> generational wealth.
>
> — *Kiana Danial*

Apply the "No-Time" Investing Method

*S*o far in this book, I've demonstrated why you don't need to do any math when investing and you don't have to take more risk than you can afford.

But now you might be thinking, *Kiana, I get it, I know I should be investing on my own, I get it that I don't have to take more risk than I can afford, and I totally see why I don't need to be a math wiz to be profitable … but I'm so busy! How on earth can I find the time to do all this?*

Congratulations, as you are in the right chapter where I'm going to show you:

How to make profitable investments in just one hour per month—even if you're super busy.

Let's go back to the Invest Diva Diamond and review the steps. Any investor first needs to identify their risk tolerance and find out where they stand financially. In other words, you need to take a minimal amount of time to set up, and you only have to do it once a year, or when something major happens in your life, like when you get married, have children, or buy a house. You can agree that this part is not an issue, right?

But you probably are worried that you have to be stuck to your screen all day in order to invest and time the markets properly, right?

The thing is that back when I first started investing, I paid closer attention to the market than I do now. I'd spend hours and hours every single day analyzing trends and trying to find the next best move, and I even used to report them for big financial companies globally.

But after I became a mom, my hands were obviously pretty full. If you're anything like me, you know how it was—my daughter was taking up 90% of my time awake, and that other 10% I was just completely exhausted.

So it was impossible to keep up the way that I used to.

What I started to do instead of being stuck to my screen all day was to check the markets once per day in one of my 15-minute milk pumping sessions while my daughter was sleeping.

So I went from hours per day to only having 15 minutes to manage my accounts. I then took it one step further and shrunk it to only once per week.

Started to Check the Markets
ONCE per day,
During ONE of My
Pumping Sessions...

114

CHAPTER TWELVE

Thankfully, I discovered a way to make all of my investments while I'm not even around.

It's called a "limit order." In a nutshell, using a limit order is kind of like using a crockpot! You just set them and forget them, then come back later and eat the profits! And let it compound over and over again.

More specifically, after using my system to identify the key psychological levels the price of your favorite asset could drop to, you go to your broker and communicate with your broker through a "buy limit order" that you want to buy this asset at that specific price. Once your limit order goes through, that means you bought that stock.

Now you are ready to sell to make a profit, right? Luckily you can use the limit order in the opposite direction as well. This is called a "sell limit order." This simply means you communicate with your broker that you want to sell your stock at a specific price, and they take care of the business for you even when you're sleeping!

Simple enough?

Let's look at some examples:

The Tesla Experiment

On August 15, 2018, way before Tesla's stock split, my system showed me that the price of Tesla stock could go down to as low as $262.

Instead of constantly checking my charts to see when the price was reached, I simply told my broker that I wanted to buy when the price hit $262. I made this communication by setting a "buy limit order" which took less than one minute. Then I went about my day, spent time with family, and focused on growing my online business.

In September 2018, my buy limit order went through at the exact price I told my broker. I instantly got a notification from my app saying that my order has been executed.

Yay! So now what do I want to do?

I want to use my system to find a good price to sell the Tesla stock with profit. Again, this doesn't have to be immediate, because remember, we are not day traders. I have plenty of time to take my next action. In fact, as my net worth grows and now that I have achieved full financial freedom, I don't even take the next step to avoid incurring capital gain taxes!

But at the time, I was still growing my account through com-

CHAPTER TWELVE

pounding my profits. I continued monitoring my portfolio once a week. On October 25, the Ichimoku indicator showed that the Tesla price had bottomed out, and my Fibonacci system (the Italian method, which I use in conjunction with the Japanese method) showed me that an optimal price to sell for a medium-risk investment was at $327.

Again, I told my app to sell Tesla at $327 by setting a "sell limit order" and went about my life.

Fast forward to December 2018 when my sell limit order went through. This means that in just a few months, I earned $65 per Tesla share.

If you had bought 100 Tesla shares with the system, you would have made $6,500 in Tesla stock just like I did.

If you do the math here, this means I earned $1,300 per minute of the time I spent doing this.

$6,500 ÷ 5 = $1,300/minute

117

Wouldn't you like to make over $1,000 per minute?

Actually, from 2017 to 2020, my system has created multiple opportunities on Tesla for me and for our Premium Investing Group (PIG) members who had medium- to high-risk tolerance, to get in and out, buy cheap, sell high, buy again low, sell again at a high price, over and over and over again, making a combined 3,000% profit.

If someone had just bought Tesla without getting in and out over the years, they would have left so much money on the table.

This is thanks to a phenomenon called the snowball effect, or compounding, which brings us to the next chapter.

Chapter Thirteen

> Compound interest
> is the eighth wonder of the world.
> He who understands it, earns it ...
> he who doesn't ... pays it.
>
> — *Albert Einstein*

Use the Zen Wealth Generator to Compound Your Money Year after Year

*S*ince Guy Spier showed me the difference between trading and investing, my personal portfolio has grown from $500 to $5,254,399.55 using the Zen Wealth Generator and the power of compounding.

I first used this to go from $500 to $50,000.

Then from $50K to $200K.

Then from $200K to $1 million.

From $1 million to over $5 million.

No matter where you are now financially, if you do these three steps, you're going to get to the next level:

>Step 1: INVEST (in yourself).

>Step 2: INCREASE (your income).

>Step 3: INVEST (in financial assets to make your money work for you).

As I demonstrated in Chapter 2, you can't achieve financial freedom and generational wealth JUST by making more money.

You also can't do it JUST by investing in the financial markets bootstrapping from zero unless you take a TON of risk which will turn you into a gambler. The reason for that is simple:

You can't make the money you don't have work for you when you're starting from zero ...

unless you have a safety net and are using debt wisely to your advantage.

But when you combine the three steps, things can move FAST without you taking too much risk. Just like it happened for our *Million Dollar Family* accelerators who are compounding on multiple levels.

Here are the stages in your Invest Diva journey:

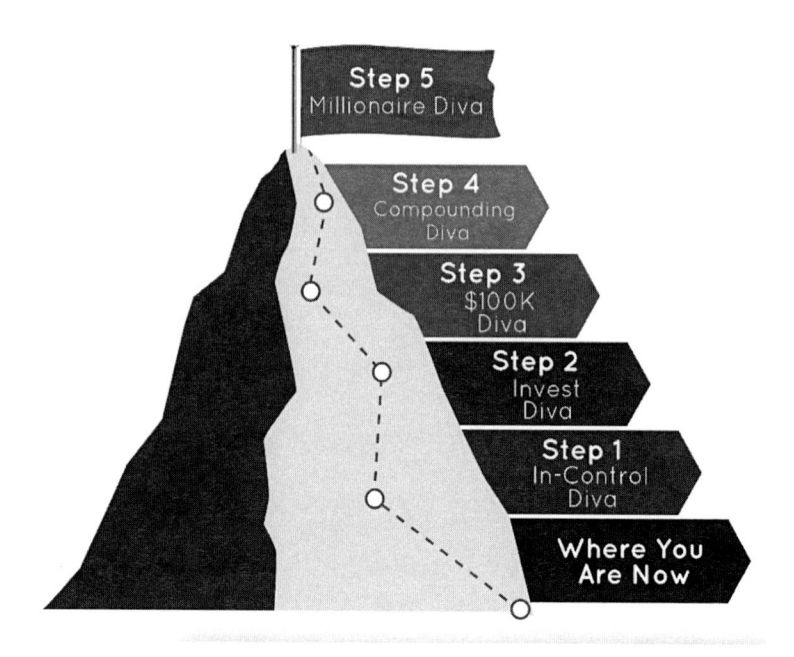

Step 5 Millionaire Diva
Step 4 Compounding Diva
Step 3 $100K Diva
Step 2 Invest Diva
Step 1 In-Control Diva
Where You Are Now

But why would you want to compound at multiple levels? So that you can collapse time frames. And the earlier you start, the better off you're going to be.

Did you know that time is NOT money? Let me prove it to you by an example I learned from my coach, Dr. Myron Golden.

If I were to give you my entire $5M portfolio right now, would you accept it?

You probably would. Right?

But what if I said, "I'll give you $5M, but only if you take your life tonight."

Would that $5M be worth it to you?

No, of course not.

Why?

Because *time* is a gazillion times more valuable than *money*.

That's why I'm kinda angry at my parents for not teaching me about money and investing early. Do you understand how much further ahead in life I would have been if I started early?

If Guy Spier had told me to stop trading and start investing before I blew out my account …

If I had learned about entrepreneurship 10 years ago …

In fact, I joke with Russell Brunson that I am very mad at him for not creating his coaching programs earlier when I had just gotten fired from my job.

Imagine ...

- How much faster I would have created a profitable business.

- How much more money I would have been able to contribute to my investment accounts.

- How many more market bull runs I would have been able to catch.

- And most important of all, how many more people I would have been able to help and prevent from going bankrupt as a result of knowing how money really works!

The money I would have made 10 years ago I would have put into my investments and it would have compounded astronomically.

Kiana, you've been talking about compounding throughout this book, but I still don't really get what you mean ...

Yes, I think I read your mind. Let's get to the definition of compounding through a series of questions:

CHAPTER THIRTEEN

How many times would a dollar have to double to reach $1 million?

Think about a $1 bill in your pocket. If it doubles, in other words, *compounds*, it will turn into $2. Once the $2 doubles, it will become $4. How many times does it have to double to reach $1 million?

You might have already guessed this.

(The answer is 20.)

That's called compounding.

Let that sink in for a second. That means if you invest $1 today and are able to double it year after year for 20 years, that dollar will turn into $1 million.

Now, of course, there's no guarantee that you can double your money every single year. But here's another question to give you some perspective.

How much money would you have after your $1 doubles 10 times?

The answer is …

$1,024.

Half the work amazingly equals less than one-tenth of 1 percent of the benefits. Can you imagine how big of a CRIME it is to become distracted and stop the doublings at this point, to purchase an XBox, a purse, or some other so-called "necessary" item?

The largest doubling is the last doubling, which is worth over half a million dollars ($524, 288) and is equal to the sum of the first 19 doublings.

Obviously, the twentieth and last doubling isn't possible without the first and smallest doubling, from one to two. When something compounds, it grows at a much more rapid rate than you expect.

Now let's get to our next question:

What's the biggest ingredient of compounding?

The answer is the T word.

It's Time.

The longer you keep reinvesting your money, the greater and more magical the compounding effect.

And that's why I'm super passionate about getting parents to do this for their children and nieces and nephews and grandkids. Because if you start doing this for them early enough, you don't even have to contribute all that much per year, but you're going to set them up to have millions of dollars when they grow up EVEN if they decide to follow their passion and become a street vocalist.

Some people call this the snowball effect.

The first time the concept of compounding really clicked for me, ironically, was when that money manager, Tim, was explaining to me how their fund works when I was in Japan.

He was actually accurate about this. The only thing that he left out was that my money was going to be locked up in their fund for 25 years, they're going to underperform the market average, and that I have to pay a 75% penalty to get my money out early.

On the positive side, I went through this experience so YOU DON'T HAVE TO. So that you can do this on your own without relying on the fund managers.

How the Snowball Effect Works

So how the snowball effect works is that you start with just a handful of the powder packed in your hands. When you put it down at the top of a hill, it doesn't seem like much.

But, to your surprise, you may end up with a much larger mass of snow by the time you get to the bottom of the hill. As the little snowball starts rolling, it can pick up additional snow as it rolls through. Then, if it keeps going, it has more surface area from which to pick up even more. The process of snow building on snow leads to compounding growth in its size.

This leads us to our final (and the scariest) question:

Do you know what else works at a compounded rate?

Your inefficient interest on your credit card debt!

The banks give you "free" credit just so they can make more money off of your money.

However, there is an amendment to this.

What if you borrowed money at high interest, but it was guaranteed to compound your money at an even higher rate?

Fun fact: There's a difference between debt vs. funding.

Debt is what Welfare Divas have. It's a liability and you use the money to buy things that don't make you money. Just like the thousands of "emotional therapy" dresses I bought when I hit rock bottom that I never wore.

On the other hand, a Millionaire Diva may take advantage of funding, if it means it's going to generate her a higher rate of return.

Funding is more like an asset.

Like when I paid for my teleprompter class. A $2,000 funding (even if I was paying 100% interest) would have generated me more money as I was getting paid $4,000 per month thanks to this new skill and was able to pay off the loan upon my first paycheck.

You can look at it this way: If you are using a loan as an investment (Zen Wealth Generator Step 1) to increase your income (Zen Wealth Generator Step 2), then you're doing it right.

Millionaire Divas leverage funding to compound.

Compounding *Bonus*

I want you to REALLY understand the power of compounding so you can even explain it to a seven-year-old. That's why I want to tell you a story from one of my most favorite books of all time, *One Grain of Rice*.

This book is taught to many Japanese kids in second grade. You can use this exact story to teach your kids about compounding and why they should start investing their money instead of buying the next XBox.

One Grain of Rice is the story of Rani, a clever girl who outsmarts a very selfish raja and saves her village. When she's offered a reward for her good deed, she asks only for one grain of rice, doubled each day for 30 days.

On the first day, Rani received only one grain of rice. The next day, two grains, and the next day, four grains. By the ninth day, she had received a total of 511 grains of rice, which doesn't look like much.

That number kept doubling until Day 30. On that day, Rani received 536,870,912 grains of rice.

Altogether, Rani had received more than one billion grains of rice.

A single decision to begin compounding ... resulted in more than one billion grains of rice!

You can do the same thing with your wealth ... and it can be effortless. It can be zen. And this will only happen once you have developed a Diva Wealth Ecosystem that we covered in Chapter 4. It's the type of wealth ecosystem where all the elements are working together to maximize your compounding.

Chapter Fourteen

> Action takers
> are
> money makers.
> — *Kiana Danial*

Increase Your Income

*C*ongratulations! You now know the basics of investing, which is one of the most important ingredients in your Diva Wealth Ecosystem.

Once our *Make Your Money Work For You PowerCourse* students graduate and start managing their portfolio like a pro, they often come to me saying how excited they are to invest, but that now they have a new problem: They don't have enough money to contribute to their portfolio to compound at an accelerated rate.

In Chapter 4, I showed you why I wasn't able to achieve Millionaire Diva status, even though I had plenty of media exposure, had written a best-selling book, and knew how to create investment strategies that outperformed the market.

The reason was that I was compounding low amounts through my investment account. But as we just covered in the previous chapter, the main ingredient in compounding through investing is TIME. Unfortunately, we as humans don't have enough of it on hand. Time is a limited commodity.

If you want to increase your income with no ceiling, an unlimited amount of money, then you must remove the time limitation. If you want to dramatically increase your net worth, you need to increase your income as much as possible in the present time, so that wealth will have a chance to compound more rapidly.

How do you do that? You take your income-producing activities to a higher level. In his book, *B.O.S.S. MOVES*[1], my coach, Myron Golden, reveals the four levels of value at which wealth is created.

The first level of value is when you attempt to create wealth by using a physical resource (i.e. your muscles) over a limited resource: time. The hardest working people who operate at this level are often the lowest paid. Think about hotel housekeeping staff, janitors, truck drivers, construction workers, painters … The list goes on.

In order to increase your level of income creation, you need to operate at the level at which money's essence exists.

Money in its essence isn't a physical being. In fact …

Money is imaginary.

Did you know that money is imaginary? Money is not a material being in its essence. You don't have to be able to touch your stocks, cryptocurrency, or credit on your credit card in order for it to have value. These assets only have value because we as a society assign value to them.

---

[1] Myron Golden, *B.O.S.S. MOVES: Business Optimization Success Secrets from a Million Dollar Round Table* (Transcendent Publishing, 2021), 37–45.

Let me ask you a question, "Which one do you think is more valuable—A gold coin (priced at $2,000 at the time of writing) or one Bitcoin (priced at $65,000 at the time of writing)?"

The answer would depend on who you ask! If you ask an alien who's just visiting the earth from a planet that's entirely made of gold instead of dirt, he would be puzzled as to why we give this "shiny dirt" any value at all!

Back to earth, if you ask Warren Buffett the same question, he'd say gold is more valuable because he doesn't *believe* in Bitcoin. And yet, we know millions of people who have become rich overnight (including myself) by investing in invisible crypto assets such as Bitcoin.

This is possible because the value of money isn't based on the material it's made of. The value of money is based on the message it carries.

The value of a stock is based on the market sentiment, which means how much confidence and *energy* the market participants have put in that asset.

Here are some other characteristics of money:

- Money holds value.

- It transfers value from one place to another.

- It converts different forms of value into others.

With this, one could argue that money is, in fact, energy.

Money is energy.

Just like a calorie is a unit of physical energy, a dollar is simply a unit of value as energy. Now that we know money is energy, we can easily see why it likes speed.

Albert Einstein discovered **E = mc²** which means energy equals mass times the speed of light squared.

Now I know I suck at math, but I had to do quantum physics for my graduation thesis in Japan. Even though I sucked at the math stuff, it did give me the logical thinking stuff, now that I think about it. So let's geek out a little bit to understand the science behind increasing your income at a higher level.

So far we know that . . .

- Money's value is dependent on the *message* it carries and that is communicated among people.
- Money is imaginary.
- Money is energy.
- Energy equals mass X the speed of light squared.

In other words …

Money = E = mc²

To increase money, we need to increase its speed twice as much as its physical representation (m).

This proves that …

Money loves speed.

No wonder why some of the wealthiest people on earth are action-takers who make fast decisions and don't let opportunities pass them by.

So the burning question that needs to be asked is, "How can we speed up our wealth creation?" In other words, "How can we operate in our human body to increase our income without limitations?"

This brings us back to Myron Golden's four levels of value, which include:

> **1. Implementation:** Making money by using a physical resource over time (i.e., janitors)
>
> **2. Unification:** Making money by using other people's physical resources over time (i.e., managers)
>
> **3. Communication:** Making money by using money's source of value, *communicating a message,* over time (i.e., salespeople)
>
> **4. Imagination:** Making money by using money's ultimate essence of being imaginary energy over time (i.e., Walt Disney)

As you reach Levels 3 and 4, your wealth creation potential goes exponentially higher.

Why? Because you're operating at the two levels of money's ESSENCE: communication and imagination.

Money's essence is made of communication and *imagination*.

Therefore, you need to operate on these two levels to speed up your wealth creation.

With this, I have scientifically proven that the only way to increase your income at a higher level, so you can enjoy your wealth while you're alive, is to operate at Myron Golden's third and fourth levels of value.

There are clearly a thousand ways to go from where you are now to unlimited income creation, which you can then compound by investing. Here are three steps that have worked for me and our Million Dollar Family students.

Step 1: Create your own business.

The first step in removing the ceiling from your income potential is breaking your ties with your 9-5. Instead of spending your time building someone else's empire, use your time to build your own empire. If you like the security of your 9-5 job, you can start by first launching your business on the side and cutting your ties fully once you have a steady income. Another method you can use is to work at companies that will give you the education you need to operate your own business.

Creating your own business also has another hidden benefit. Even if you have a 9-5 job, having your business will help you with tax deductions, especially in capitalist countries such as the US, which rewards entrepreneurship with tax write-offs.

To get a free downloadable PDF guide to the State Corporation Commission (SCC) link for each state in the US or to find out how to create an LLC/S-Corporation in another country, go to Earn.InvestDiva.com.

Step 2: Use your mouth (or mouth equivalents).

Whether you're in e-commerce, coaching, or tech, you need to use your mouth to operate at a higher level of value (communication).

An educated customer is a loyal customer.

If you don't use your mouth to educate and connect with your customers, even if you're in e-commerce, you'll become a commodity and have to start dropping your prices to compete in the marketplace.

But if you figure out your niche and communicate to move them, they will never go to your competition no matter how much of a discount they'd get elsewhere.

If you're committed to your 9-5 job, seek out roles where you can use your communication skills to remove or increase your wage ceiling.

Now you might be saying, "But Kiana! I'd rather die than speak in public!"

To which I'd respond:

Get comfortable with being uncomfortable. You're reading this book to learn the Million Dollar Family Secrets, but the *REAL* secret lies within you.

YOU have to become the kind of person that does the things other people don't. That's the only way you can achieve the results they haven't achieved.

Furthermore, thanks to technology, we can also convey our message with our fingers, with sign language, or any part of our body that can convey a message.

Thanks to technology, even people who literally can't use any of their body parts—like the late Stephen Hawking (the smartest man alive until 2018, RIP)—can use technology to communicate.

So don't let your Welfare Diva mentality give you any excuses.

Step 3: Use your imagination.

We proved in this chapter that money is imaginary, and in order to operate at its highest level you need to use your imagination. When you combine your imagination with your communication skills, (which you can TOTALLY develop even if you weren't born with them), you can operate at the level at which fortunes are made.

Get in touch with your inner child. Meditate. Write a book.

Becoming an author is one of my favorite ways to start an impactful business. Not only will it add to your social proof (being an *author* gives you *authority*) but it also opens doors for meaningful partnerships and interviews that can contribute to your influence.

Increasing your influence is the final element of the Diva Wealth Ecosystem. It has helped many of our Million Dollar Family Accelerator students jumpstart their business, turning their passion into a tangible money-making machine.

Just reached my $10K milestone! Feeling grateful. #divawin

—Grace W.

Chapter Fifteen

> You don't get in life what you want, you get what you are. Become the kind of person who can live the life of your dreams.

— *Kiana Danial*

Increase Your Influence

*I*was eight years old when I first decided I wanted to become a well-known author. I remember reading Jean Webster's novel *Daddy Long Legs* and being inspired by the main character Jerusha Abbot, an orphan who aspired to become an author and eventually did. As a kid, I thought the ultimate success was becoming an author.

As I grew up and watched American singers and actors on our satellite TV, I thought the key to success was becoming famous. In my head, fame would directly translate into wealth, which was what I was longing for all along growing up.

It wasn't until a few years after I came to the US that I found out fame alone doesn't get people to wealth. I experienced it firsthand.

A couple of years into my Invest Diva journey, and after publishing my very first book, *Invest Diva's Guide to Making Money in Forex*, I landed my very first TV appearance to talk about my book on CNN International. A true dream come true especially since CNN International along with BBC were the two international news sources we had in Iran where I grew up. I thought the moment I stepped out of the studio after being on air, I would magically make over a million dollars and become an instant best-selling author.

But what happened instead, was this:

A very proud mom, and almost zero additional book sales.

I was puzzled and started looking into famous people's net worth and financial situations. I soon found out that there are two types of famous people:

- Famous and in debt
- Famous and in charge

I learned about A-list singers who were massively in debt, like Lady Gaga who was $3 million in the hole after her Monster Ball tour. Or Johnny Depp who was drowning in $100 million debt. I then started looking into social media influencers with millions of followers online who also fit in the same two categories.

Those who were just famous without a Diva Wealth Ecosystem were not only broke but often in debt. But those who were able to fit their influence in a perfectly structured wealth ecosystem were accelerating their portfolio at the speed of a rocketship.

While many influencers are broke, if done correctly, increasing your influence can compound your wealth at an increasingly accelerated rate.

For me, the breakthrough came about after I decided to be intentional with my influence. Instead of one-hit wonders on national TV, I decided to share my journey on social media and speak directly to the pain of the people I was called to serve: moms who wanted to take control of their financial future and create generational wealth.

CHAPTER FIFTEEN

The moment I switched my mindset from "wanting to become famous" to "wanting to serve through influence" I went viral and sales started coming through, taking me from zero to a million in less than a year.

If you think about it, the same happens with big corporations. The most successful businesses of all time have consistently been in the business of serving and wowing their customers. Think Apple, Disney, and Tesla. Each of these businesses has an influencer with charisma: Steve Jobs, Walt Disney, Elon Musk. These business owners have moved the masses to the point that even if their products are not as good as the competition, people won't switch.

People are the heart and soul of any successful business. That is why large companies like Facebook and Microsoft pay billions of dollars to acquire companies like Whatsapp and Skype.

Both Whatsapp and Skype are very basic communication tools. Facebook and Microsoft could knock off the technology in-house and build a similar, if not better, software for a minimal amount.

However, Microsoft purchased Skype back in 2011 and paid $8.5 BILLION for it. Facebook purchased Whatsapp for $21.8 billion and they considered it cheap. Why?

By paying $21.8 billion for Whatsapp, Facebook essentially paid only $55 per user, which is a MUCH cheaper cost per acquisition than I have to pay Facebook when running ads.

Now, remember my $5 million portfolio? We also have 155K contacts in our list of subscribers.

If I were held for ransom tomorrow and was asked to give them either my 155K contact list or my $5 million portfolio, which one do you think I'd choose?

I'd give up the portfolio. People are where it's at.

Money is imaginary. But people are real.

I wouldn't even shed a tear if I lost my $5M portfolio. Ok, maybe I'd cry a little bit. But I know that I'd be able to rebuild my fortune faster than I built it the first time because of the person I've become, the skills I've acquired, and the following I've created.

In fact, we haven't *just* created a following ... we have built a community of people. I have produced results for almost 3,000 in our *Make Your Money Work For You* PowerCourse alone. We've over-delivered with more coaching, answering all questions, picking you up when you're down, celebrating your wins.

So now if I lose all my money, I still have my people. I have their results. I know exactly how to do this all over again, and it'll probably take me much less time this time around because I've done it before and because my people are there.

At the beginning of this book, I quoted "the best time to start investing was 20 years ago and the second-best is today."

The same thing can be said about your influence over a network of people.

The best time to start building your influence was 20 years ago.

The second-best time is today.

One of the fastest and most effective ways I've seen to help my students build a personal influence is to become an author. After taking my Two-Day Author Method (which is the method I used to write this book, by the way), many new business owners have created impact and influence through their books. Then, they take the components of their book, slice them up into smaller pieces, and repurpose them on social media to compound their influence.

When it comes to social media, there are two types of people: content consumers versus content creators. Which type do you think you need to become to achieve influence?

10 Myths and Lies About Increasing Your Influence

When I talk to pre-entrepreneurs about the importance of increasing their influence, I'm often faced with a lot of resistance. They have quite a few misconceptions about the role of influencers and how they affect your business. Let's grow your business by busting through some of these myths.

Myth NO. 1

You need to have a HUGE following to monetize it.

Incorrect. It's the quality versus the quantity. I've seen business owners with only 1,000 followers making thousands of dollars through their influence because they had a niched-down following. Your number of followers may not be that large, but as long as they are the exact type of people you are looking to serve, you are creating an influence over them.

The opposite is also true, which brings us to Myth #2:

Myth NO. 2

If you have a million followers, you'll become a millionaire.

Wrong. The majority of "influencers" with millions of followers are struggling to make ends meet. Influence alone cannot operate your Diva Wealth Ecosystem. But combined with the other components, it'll take you to generational wealth quicker than you thought.

Myth NO. 3

You need to show your face to create a following.

I understand that some people may have anxiety over showing their face on social media. Maybe they are worried about privacy. Maybe they don't like the way they sound. Well, I've got good news for you. There are thousands of influencers on social media, such as Instagram, Facebook, and even YouTube, who never show their faces, but have been able to amass millions of followers who are also turning into paying customers.

One of my friends, Paula @WomanCEOMindset is a great example of this. In one year, she reached over 800K hard-core followers on Instagram (who are ready to throw their wallets at her every time she drops a new product)—without ever showing her face.

Myth NO. 4

You need to be on all social media channels.

You don't need to, and in fact, I don't recommend it when you're getting started. For me, TikTok was the one that made me blow out during the Covid-19 lockdown. So I stuck with it. I still create the majority of my content on TikTok and then repurpose the same content on other social media. You can do the same. Focus on one thing. Repurpose if possible.

Myth NO. 5

You need to be perfect.

You need to know that authenticity is where it's at. Many people see influencers' polished and very perfect stories and videos and think that's the type of content they need to make to create a following. In my experience, creating true influence is only possible through authenticity.

The word "perfect" doesn't even exist. It's just an opinion. And almost no one, (even the most influential influencers), starts there. Just show up and start doing it and you will get better.

Myth NO. 6

It's going to take a lot of your time.

If you follow me on social media you probably know that I have been consistently publishing content on a daily basis. This doesn't mean I spend hours every day crafting and publishing the content.

For my video content, I have dedicated one day per week when I put on makeup and create the videos. Throughout the day, every time I'm inspired by a quote in a book, or if I think of something cool to share with my audience, I simply add them to what I call my "content treasury box." This can be a simple word document, a Slack threat, or a Voxer channel where you can stack your creative ideas as they come to you during your workout session, in the shower, during a meeting, or while you're scrolling social media on the potty.

Some weeks you may be slow and some weeks you may have your creative juices oozing out of you to the point that you make a whole month's worth of content in one day… and then all you have to do is to take 30 minutes per day publishing on your social media of choice.

My biggest advice for creating an influence is to set a publishing frequency that matches your lifestyle and STICK with it.

If you think you can't stick to publishing daily, then stick with publishing weekly.

Marie Forleo, one of the most successful female entrepreneurs in America, only publishes once a week. This has enabled her to focus on quality over quantity and create raving fans. But she has stuck with it for over 15 years.

Social media experts like Rachel Pederson publish 3–5 times per day. She, too, has reached the level of influence that can turn into an increased income.

Myth NO. 7

If you give your best stuff away on social media, people won't buy your paid stuff.

WRONG. You HAVE to give away your best stuff on social media. In fact, you must only publish things on social media that you COULD have charged for. Publishing low-quality content is the best way to tell people that you can't deliver and they shouldn't pay you.

Long gone are the days when information alone was what people were searching for. With an overwhelming amount of information on the Internet, people are now looking for filters and coaches who can help them EXECUTE on the information.

That's why giving away your best information for free won't hurt your income. People will trust that you know what you're talking about, and will then pay you to help them execute on the information to create the actual results they're looking for.

When I run an online masterclass or challenge, for example, such as our *"Start Building Your Wealth Challenge"* (YourWealthNow.com) I don't leave anything off the table. I dive deep into our students' personal questions and even technical questions. I prove to them that I can help them by *actually helping them.*

In fact, the content I share in these trainings are things I either paid hundreds of thousands of dollars to learn or spent YEARS in trial and error to learn.

I share all the information for free or at a minimal price to show my followers that I can help them find their own way to get out of their own way and move the needle the fastest towards a million-dollar portfolio.

Once people know and trust you through your influence, they will then buy your stuff because …

- They want to get access to you.

- They want to get access to your stuff (if you're in e-commerce).

- They don't want the education to stop.

- They want you to hold their hand.

- They want it structured in one place.

- They need to do the thing in order to master it.

You can't master by scrolling through random content. All you're doing is giving yourself a dopamine hit. Your brain THINKS you're learning. But you retain ONLY 10% of what you hear UNLESS you do something and do it over and over again until you MASTER it.

I have given away almost all of the PowerCourse modules on TikTok but the ones who have seen them all, are also the ones who eventually become our highest-paid students.

Let me ask you this, if you wanted to learn how to become a double-diamond skier, you might read the best-selling book, *Ultimate Skiing* by Ron LeMaster. But then would you get on a ski lift, go to the top of the mountain, and start skiing down that super steep double-black-diamond slope?

How would you feel at the top of that mountain? Would you have the expertise you need to get down that slope from just reading the book? Would you look like a professional skier or would you fall on that first mogul and then roll all the way down the mountain?

People need to do the thing in order to master it. And most people don't want to do it alone. So don't be afraid to give away your best stuff. Once you establish yourself as the expert, people will want to buy more and more because they appreciate your expertise. They see how valuable you are as you help them reach their goals and get the results they desire.

Myth NO. 8

Your audience isn't on social media.

Yes, they are! All you have to do is to find out where they're congregating and influence them through the channel they are spending most of their time in.

CHAPTER FIFTEEN

Myth NO. 9

You have a corporate job, so you can't.

Having influence is not taboo. You don't have to post inappropriate photos of yourself to gain influence if that's not the field you work in. But you certainly can use the power of influence to accelerate your corporate job.

When you create your own content, you control the conversation, and you influence the world's impression of you.

A perfect example of this is Preeti, a member of our Million Dollar Family Accelerator program. She recently received a job offer as a direct result of the content that she had been creating and consistently posting online. The company was so impressed with her ability and desire to empower other women that they now want her to do the same for their employees. Opportunity found HER because she chose to apply what she has learned, share her knowledge, and control the conversation.

If you are creating content, you may attract better, higher income through another job offer, and you may attract customers just by being a recognizable authority in your space.

Myth NO. 10

You're scared of trolls.

Have you ever watched Jimmy Kimmel's segment where he gets celebrities to read "Mean Tweets" that were posted about them on social media? It's one of my favorite things to watch because 1) it shows that no matter how awesome and influential you become, you're always going to have haters, and 2) it's your attitude toward the people who don't like you that will raise you even higher in front of your fans, turning them into hard-core fans.

One of the best things that happens on my social media posts is negative comments. Not only does it help open up the conversation, but it also increases my level of "like" and "trust" in front of my fans. It helps those who were on the fence about me to pick a side and either become a hater or a fan.

For our Million Dollar Family Accelerators, we actually have an award for when they get their first negative comment because that shows that they're creating a feeling and influence among their audience.

If you're not pissing anybody off, you're not gaining hard-core fans.

Trolls are good. Stop with the excuses and do it now.

Chapter Sixteen

> Money is always eager
> and ready to work
> for anyone who is ready
> to employ it.
>
> — *Idowu Koyenikan*

Create an Automated Active Income

So far in this book, we have covered a whole lot about investing. But we have also mentioned the importance of building a Diva Wealth Ecosystem and increasing your income so that you can invest more.

We briefly touched on the levels at which you should be operating on, in order to increase your income, in Chapter 14. I also mentioned how I was able to create an automated active income by building an automated funnel in Chapter 4.

While getting into the details of creating a funnel goes far beyond the scope of this book, I did want to share the example of how I made it happen for me and the fundamentals that helped me along the way. That way, you may have enough inspiration to apply it to your situation and turn your passion into a cash machine just like I did.

Please also note that some of the tactics I used for my automated funnel could be outdated in the future but the fundamentals of the process are timeless. That's why I'll be focusing on them in this chapter.

> *As a gift to you, we will be offering further guidance at earn.investdiva.com. You can also contact us at learn@investdiva.com for assistance.*

Creating Your Offer

As Alex Hormozi puts it in his book, *$100M Offers*[2] ...

"The *only* way to conduct business is through a value exchange, a trade of dollars for value."

Your offer is the lifeblood of your business.

Your income will only increase as high as the value that your offer creates for the people who need it and have the ability to pay for it.

Did you notice what I just said?

I said, "for the people who need it and have the ability to pay for it."

This means your offer has a lot to do with the people who you're serving.

Without having a "good who" (i.e. ideal clients) no matter how good your offer is, you won't make any money.

Your offer needs to resolve a very specific, yet profound pain for your ideal customers.

When I first learned how funnels can help me turn my offer into a lucrative online business, I didn't wait. I invested in the

---

[2] Alex Hormozi, *$100M Offers: How To Make Offers So Good People Feel Stupid Saying No* (Acquisition.com LLC, 2021).

best coaches to teach me how I could turn my passion into cash. I took it a little too far though. I became so excited about funnels that I practically went "Funnel Crazy." I launched a total of 145 funnels and I was still making no money.

Clearly, I got frustrated and took to my coaching program's Facebook page to vent.

> I'm taking action on ALL things. Where's my Two Comma Club Award?!!

I said, "I'm taking action on ALL things. Where's my Two Comma Club Award[3]?!" To which my coach, Russell Brunson (the co-founder of ClickFunnels), responded: "You're doing too much. Focus on ONE thing."

He said that the easiest and fastest way to a million-dollar revenue is to run Facebook ads to a webinar funnel. More specifically, run Facebook ads to one group of people to help resolve one valuable painful problem.

---

[3] The Two Comma Club Award is an award given by ClickFunnels to customers who make one million dollars or more through one funnel.

Now, I had to make a decision. Who are the people I want to help the most? Who are the people that one of my solutions is the most valuable for?

I had recently become a mom and my whole world had become about my daughter. For the first two years of her life, I felt my life was completely out of my control.

I knew I wasn't alone. Most moms I met felt they were losing control of everything. One of the most important things moms—and women in general—stop focusing on is their own financial future. Statistically, women live longer than men, and not being financially independent is something that catches up with us when it's too late.

It's important to start investing early on behalf of your children. As I mentioned earlier, if you contribute just $50 per month to your child's investment account, that will set them up for life. But most moms don't know this and aren't doing this.

It was standing right there looking at me. It was my calling. I finally knew what to do. I wanted to help moms take control of their financial future.

I focused all of my marketing activities on just that group of people. To my surprise, even though I had narrowed down my audience, my TikTok, Instagram, and other social media accounts grew exponentially.

These social media accounts are much more powerful tools than just media exposure on TV because I learned that it's very hard to get people to go to your funnel while you're on TV; whereas, social media allows you to directly plug into your funnel.

This made my wealth ecosystem even more powerful. Once I had a specific funnel that solved a specific and significant problem for a specific group of people, I quickly earned my first million dollars in my funnel which earned me my first Two Comma Club Award.

Selecting Your Ideal Customers

Your offer is only as good as the receiving end. If you offer the best homemade eight-course French meal to your brother who just had three McDonald's hamburgers, a bag full of chips, and a large Coke, not only is he not going to appreciate your eight-course cuisine, he might straight-up end up in the bathroom instead.

Your customers must actually need your offer. Otherwise, it has no value for them and therefore you won't make any money.

The good news is, you are in control of who you decide to work with. The most important step in your business (that most businesses fail to take) is to identify a starving crowd.

That way, even if you have a mediocre offer and horrific sales skills, chances are you're going to be able to serve your customers and increase your income.

Another good news is that you don't have to serve the whole world. In fact, you absolutely should not. As the saying goes

The riches are in the niches.

This may sound counter-intuitive when you first hear it. But the more you niche down and focus on a very specific group of people, the more money you'll make.

When I first started my Invest Diva business, I wanted to help everyone and anyone take control of their financial future. While this may *sound* great, I soon realized that no one was really listening to me because I wasn't calling anyone out. I was like a random person on the subway shouting out random things to random people without really considering their needs.

Once I decided to niche down and serve "stay-at-home moms of toddlers" my business took a significant jump. That's pretty specific compared to "moms" or "anyone who pays me."

Could I have helped all the other people? Of course I could have. But to maintain my offer's focus, (especially as someone who was just starting out and not quite as influential as others who were offering similar services in my marketplace), knowing *exactly* who my offer was for was a game changer.

It helped me create TikTok and Instagram content that spoke *exactly* to moms of toddlers and made them stop and watch me pitch my offer because they could instantly see that I could solve the *exact* problem they were having as new moms who are feeling they've lost control of everything.

Pricing Your Offer

The price you put on your offer has a direct correlation with the value it creates for your ideal customer.

Warren Buffett said: "Price is what you pay. Value is what you get."

The biggest mistake businesses make, on the other hand, is to lower their price in order to increase the perceived value of their offer. I first learned this from my coach Russell Brunson. Lowering your price to remain competitive is the surest and fastest way to destroy your business and ensure you're serving nobody.

Imagine if someone in your family had a critical heart problem. Would you go on Google and search "heart surgeon on sale"? Or will you type in "Best heart surgeon near me?"

Dan Kennedy, a legendary marketer once said: "There is no strategic benefit to being the second cheapest in the marketplace, but there is for being the most expensive."

If you're the best, no one expects you to be the cheapest. If you're the cheapest, no one believes that you're the best.

I say all this to prepare you for the formula I use for pricing my offers. I typically calculate how much time/ money/ pain I can save my customers with my offer. This is literally the "value" of my offer and it must be at least 10 times more than the price of your offer.

So if I know with certainty that I can help our students make at least $20,000 in the markets following my strategy and that it is going to help them avoid paying hundreds of thousands of dollars in commission fees to money managers and penalties for early withdrawals of their funds, then I'd price my offer at least $2K.

I am certain about this because we have seen our students make 100 times more than this by just their initial investment in us. So while some may perceive a $2K offer as a high ticket item, it is a huge discount compared to the value that we create for them.

This doesn't limit your offer to the wealth category.

If you are in the health and nutrition market, for example, you can calculate the health benefits of your offer that can prevent your ideal clients from becoming overweight, getting heart disease, and shortening their life expectancy.

If you're in the relationship space, you can calculate how much emotional pain you're going to save a couple who are heading for divorce, the amount they'd be paying to therapy, to divorce lawyers, and worst of all, the emotional toll it could take on their children.

The biggest takeaway from this section is this: Instead of lowering the price of your offer, increase its value for your ideal customer. Not only will you increase your income faster, but you'll also create raving fans and customer success stories that will help you grow your business even faster.

Naming Your Offer

Once you know exactly whose pain you are resolving with your offer, you can now get creative with naming your offer.

We're not talking about the name of your company here. We're talking about the name of the unique service you're offering.

You must appropriately name your offer to attract the right customer to the right offer. Powerful names for customers who have never heard of you could include your customer's deepest pain, and move them away from it.

Examples:
- 7 Biggest Mistakes New Moms Should Avoid
- 5 Biggest Pitfalls New Investors Fall For
- 3 Biggest Mistakes Millennials Make When Working Out

If your customer is already fairly familiar with you and your offer (we call them a hot audience in the marketing world) you can give your offer a name that moves them towards pleasure.

Examples (these are some of the programs we offer at Invest Diva and have had success with):

- The 2-Day Author Method for Entrepreneurs
- Make Your Money Work For You PowerCourse
- Million Dollar Family Accelerator
- Start Building Your Wealth Challenge

Selling Your Offer

One of the most valuable things I learned from my coach, Eileen Wilder, was the power of charging your customers. When I first hired her, I had the biggest limiting belief about sales that I burst out crying when she said I need to charge my mastermind students thousands of dollars. My Welfare Diva mentality was coming at me in full force and I was crying, shedding real tears saying, "I can't sell. And I don't want to sell."

In my head, and thanks to my upbringing, charging for my offer was something bad I was doing *to* my students.

Can you relate to this? I want to ask you a question and keep it real with me ...

Do you have a hard time with the concept of selling?

The reason you don't like selling is that you think that selling is getting somebody to do something that they don't want to do, to buy something that they don't want to buy, and spend some money that they don't want to spend, right?

That's when my coach reminded me of something that I had never noticed before—and that was the amount of joy salespeople actually create.

Are you shocked that I just said that? It's because when we say salespeople, you only remember those sleazy salespeople who try to convince you to buy something you don't want.

So let me ask you a question. Have you ever received a birthday gift? Or a Christmas present you absolutely loved? Do you remember as a child how happy you got to get that new pair of shoes? Later in life, an iPhone?

Here's the thing. If somebody somewhere hadn't sold that for a profit, first of all, our whole economy would have collapsed, and second, you wouldn't have anything.

If it wasn't for salespeople, you wouldn't have a fridge, a washing machine, a dishwasher, a car, books, cups, forks, plates.

Nothing. We'd be in a cave killing each other for entertainment. Salespeople are, in fact, the heartbeat of our economy. Money needs to be in motion just like water; otherwise, it goes bad and economies collapse.

My COO and I were invited to a work event in Florida and we thought it was going to be a sit-down dinner. I had my stylist get me this little black dress ... I had my red-bottom high heels on ... My COO had this beautiful dress with her high heels ... We were ready to be fancy ... until the host surprised us by dropping us off at ... Universal Orlando!

They had rented out the whole Harry Potter land and we had to walk around 20 minutes to get to the venue IN OUR HIGH HEELS.

We were in tears. Blisters all over our feet, and we had to also walk that distance back in our heels.

Can you imagine how thankful I was to see a stand open that late at night with some guy selling flip-flops?!

Do you know how much I was willing to pay him to get me out of that misery?

Selling isn't doing something **to** people. That's the type of salesperson you DON'T want to be.

That's why we say find your people, ask them what THEY want, and then give it to them.

We don't say, go find something to sell and then force it down the throat of people who don't want it. Selling is creating value for a profit for someone who already wants it!

And since people don't take free stuff seriously and don't value it, you'd be doing them a disservice if you don't charge them because …

People who pay, pay attention.

Grace is one of our Million Dollar Family students from Australia, and during Covid, her optometry practice had to shut down.

She has now not only grown her portfolio by over 100% but she was also able to quit her job, write a book, create her own coaching business, and change other people's lives. She's been sharing her testimonials with us, the number of other people's lives she's been changing as a result of the ripple effect of investing in herself and somebody, (me), selling her something.

Do you think Grace would have been better off staying in optometry in Australia which, by the way, was still in lockdown?

So don't buy into the lie that our collective cultures try to perpetrate on us that when you sell something to somebody, you're doing something bad to them.

If you have something of value to offer, you have a moral obligation to do everything in your power to offer it to them at a price that makes them pay attention and take you seriously.

Automating Your Offer

There has never been an easier time to make automated active income. Thanks to the Internet (and now Web 2.0 and Web 3.0) we have more opportunities than ever to create automated systems that sell our offers on auto-pilot and create even more value for your customers.

The way I was able to automate one of my income streams was using Russell Brunson's *Perfect Webinar* funnel.

Here are the steps I took to automate this funnel:

- Did the presentation LIVE once to see how the audience perceived it and if it had a satisfactory conversion rate for my offer

- Uploaded the recording to our website using a system called "WebinarJam." This system allows me to run the webinar every 15 minutes.

- Hired 24/7 support team to answer the questions of a live audience

- Automated my ads to bring more of my customers to that funnel

Voila! This automated webinar is making us at least $500K per month. See exactly how it works here: learn.investdiva.com.

With the advent of Web 3.0, we are potentially going to have even more opportunities to create higher value for our customers and automate the whole process so we don't have to sell our time but can still create an amazing experience for them.

Final Thoughts

My automated webinar funnel has become the cash-cow machine for my investment accounts. And through the power of investing, the money that I made on our webinar funnel has allowed us to consider buying our dream house either in Hawaii or in New York (we still haven't decided on the location at the time of writing, but it's nice to have options, isn't it?).

I'm not telling you this to impress you. I'm trying to impress upon you right now, to begin to see that if you believe in yourself enough to take action on all the things you're learning in this book, this is possible for you.

> *Bonus:*
> Go to Earn.InvestDiva.com to grab my Money Magnet Journal.

When I signed up for the power course a year ago, I had NO idea what effect that would have on my life. It changed how I look at investing, growing wealth, and money.

Today I realized that my stock portfolio + crypto portfolio = a little bit over $100K!!! I can't wait to see it in 5 or 10 years! Thank you, Kiana Danial.

—Edyta A.

Chapter Seventeen

> Once you believe
> you can do something,
> there is not a single person
> in the universe who can
> convince you otherwise.
>
> — *Germany Kent*

Create Generational Wealth

I wrote this book with one goal in mind: to show you the roadmap to create generational wealth through the Diva Wealth Ecosystem by using the Zen Wealth Generator as your tool.

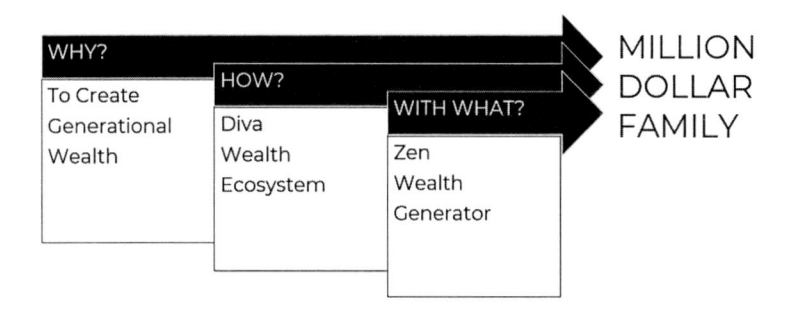

WHY?	HOW?	WITH WHAT?	→	MILLION DOLLAR FAMILY
To Create Generational Wealth	Diva Wealth Ecosystem	Zen Wealth Generator		

Have you ever wondered how much money you need to make to never have to work again?

We call this financial freedom, which is the step you must achieve before you can create generational wealth.

Despite the popular misconception that you need to aim for a specific dollar amount in savings (like $1 million), the real question is how much income you're going to have.

This is how you can calculate the amount of money you need in your investment portfolio to NEVER have to work again:

Step 1: Get your annual expenses. Add everything from rent to food, vacations you typically take in a year, and any other outbound cash flow, and sum them up using your phone's calculator.

Step 2: Divide the number by 0.04.

Voila! Once you hit this number in your investment account—NOT savings account—you can declare financial freedom.

This is called the 4% rule. While the number is not precise and is due to fluctuate based on inflation, if your diversified investment account simply does a bare minimum of 8% growth per year, you can assume you've achieved financial freedom.

The cool thing is, the 4% rule assumes you increase your spending every year by the rate of inflation—not on how your portfolio performs—so whether or not you're doubling your money every year or just barely keeping up with the market average, this could work!

You hit this number at 30? Great! You can stop working.

But how can you accelerate your rate of return? And better yet:

How long will it take for your investment to double?

Here's another cool trick to find out what the average rate of return you're going to need to double your money in a certain amount of time. It's called The Rule of 72.

This is a simple way to give you an estimate of how long an investment will take to double if you're expecting a fixed annual rate of interest. It's not 100% accurate but gives you an idea so you can create your financial plans accordingly.

If you divide 72 by the rate of return you're expecting on an annual basis, you can get a rough understanding of how many years it will take for your initial investment to double.

It tells you that if you put your money in a savings account that gives you a 2% return per year, it's going to take you 36 years for your $100 to turn into $200!

That sucks, right? What the heck!

In 36 years, I'm going to be retired somewhere. What am I going to do with that $200?!

And that's how you know that this is not a good rate of return on your investment, which gives you another reason why you need to immediately move your cash from your savings account to an investment account.

If you want your money to grow faster, you've got to get a higher return than just 2%.

Even if you put your money in the S&P 500 and get an average 8% return, the rule of 72 says it's going to take you nine years to double your money (72/8%=9).

That is way better than the savings account, right?

Rule of 72

At 2% return: → 72/ 2% = 36 years
At 8% return: → 72/8% = 9 years
At 35% return: → 72/ 35% = 2 years

In the past five years, we've been able to average a minimum of 50% return on our portfolio, but let's stay conservative and say the average is 35%.

At an average 35% return per year, your money is going to double every two years.

If you want to double your money every year, you need to have a 100% return.

Want to know a secret?

In some years we've had a 200% return, and with some assets, we've had over 3,000% return, which has been crazy.

Combine these returns with high income and you'd become the true definition of a jackpot.

This also shows the power of compounding and the importance of choosing your assets wisely ... and actually selling once you hit your desired rate of return if you're not consistently contributing to your portfolio for compounding purposes.

The beauty of compounding is that you don't even have to be doubling or 10Xing your money in order for it to reach millions. But even more fascinating is that:

It takes the same natural energy for something to double from 1 to 2, as it takes for it to go from $268,435,456 to $536,870,912.

The only difference is the amount of time you're giving your money to work for you and grow, while you're doing the things you love.

"If you don't find a way to make money while you sleep, you will work until you die."

—Warren Buffett

With the Invest Diva Movement, our mission is not just to help people achieve financial freedom in their lifetime …

We're here to help you create GENERATIONAL WEALTH by compounding not only on your investments but throughout your whole Diva Wealth Ecosystem that has all the necessary elements to automate your wealth creation so that:

Your money makes more money, and the money that money makes, also makes money.

For me, once I found the missing element in my Diva Wealth Ecosystem, generational wealth was inevitable. I had the expertise, I had the books, I had the influence, and I was compounding the little money I was making. But once I created an automated online offer, my Diva Wealth Ecosystem was completed and resulted in exponential compounding in my investing accounts.

Let me ask you a question. Would you like the income that

you make from your offer and funnel to have exponential growth like that?

I would like to encourage you to start imagining this in your head: Imagine that your money is making more and more money for you in the background, turning into this massive avalanche of money!

The reason why I want you to visualize this money avalanche is because one of the most powerful things that helped me achieve my goals has been manifestation.

In 2020, I was in the audience at Funnel Hacking LIVE, listening to Tony Robbins as he brought fire on the stage. That's when I drew this picture on my notepad:

CHAPTER SEVENTEEN

You may agree that drawing is not my top talent, but what I meant and could clearly envision in my head was being on the same stage where Tony Robbins was speaking. In my speech, I was talking to the crowd about making their money work for them.

A year later …

I got introduced as one of the speakers at Funnel Hacking LIVE 2021! The privilege of sharing the same stage as Tony Robbins and getting to speak in front of thousands of entrepreneurs is one of the most powerful manifestations I have ever brought to reality. If you can believe it, you can achieve it. I'm living proof!

As we wrap up this book, I'd like to show you how each class of people in our society deals with money differently:

- The poor deal with it on a day-to-day basis.
- Low income: week to week.
- Middle class: month to month.
- Rich: year to year.
- Affluent: decade to decade.
- Truly wealthy people: generation to generation.

Which one of these classes are you in right now?

What is the next action you need to take that will turn the needle the most toward generational wealth?

"It's not how much money you make, but how much money you keep, how hard it works for you, and how many generations you keep it for."

—Robert Kiyosaki

This quote by Robert Kiyosaki beautifully sums up the whole wealth creation formula, and I've found out that it is only possible by creating a Diva Wealth Ecosystem where you have all the elements necessary to sustain your wealth through your lifetime and beyond.

- You can't get there just by increasing your investments (without increasing your income).

- You can't get there just by increasing your income (without investing).

- You can't get there just by increasing your influence (without increased income and investments).

Even if you're a high level entrepreneur, even if you're making six, seven, or eight figures per year, you still need to be in control of your finances. Remember:

Personal finance is personal.

As much as you may be tempted to defer your portfolio to

someone else, this may be the one task you should consider doing yourself.

Even if you eventually decide to hire a money manager to do it for you, you need to understand the basics so they can't take advantage of you.

After all, no one cares more about your money than you do.

If you're serious about creating generational wealth without having to work until the day you die, you need to start making your money work for you today and create a Diva Wealth Ecosystem that lubricates and accelerates your compounding.

The time to take control of your financial future is now.

Acknowledgments

I want to thank all the brilliant value investors and the financial experts I have learned from who have helped me get to where I am today.

With extreme gratitude, my thanks goes to Russell Brunson for showing me the other side of wealth creation. Thank you for helping me get my message out to hundreds of thousands of people who need financial literacy. Also, for having faith in me to ask me to speak at your event. You are impacting millions of people and are truly one of a kind. I can never thank you enough.

I want to thank Jennifer Ashkenazy for literally discovering me, and helping me publish my very first book with McGraw-Hill in 2012. You opened the door that has led to the success of Invest Diva today.

A special thanks goes to Paul Mladjenovic for trusting me with the *Cryptocurrency Investing for Dummies* book, which opened a whole new world both to me and my audience as a result.

I want to thank my good friend Nathaniel Hansen for always cheering me on and for having my back in this male-dominated field of finance.

My thanks goes to Bob Proctor, who never ceases to inspire and who leads by example. Thank you for taking the time to write a testimonial for this book on very short notice.

A special thanks goes to Myron Golden for not only writing a testimonial for this book but also for building up my confidence and showing me better ways to inspire.

I want to thank Eileen Wilder for making me comfortable with the art of selling and showing me why selling is serving.

I want to thank Guy Spier for helping me get out of the day trading misery and showing me the light of value investing and the methods of Warren Buffett.

I want to thank my husband Matt for being the most amazing dad which allowed me to focus on our investments and our businesses.

A very special thanks goes to our entire Invest Diva team—especially Tristan Craig, Jacqui Short, Arleny Lopez-Cordero, Edyta Awan, Fabiola Urrutia, Geetika Chitlangia, Maria Nawatani, Johana Paula Cabante, Danah Regine Danlag, and Ketti Ciarniello. You not only kept the company running while I locked myself away to finish this book, but you also gave me the motivation and the assistance to have one of the fastest turnarounds on any book. Thank you for believing in our mission.

I want to thank Michael Mejido for helping me get my message out in the major media outlets.

Finally, a very special thanks goes to Lori Lynn and her team (especially Mary Rembert and Shanda Trofe) for taking on this project even though we were on an insane deadline of only a week to finish this book. Thank you, Lori, for making sure every single word was finely tuned. You are the best editor I

ACKNOWLEDGMENTS

have had the pleasure of working with and the true definition of a superhuman.

Most importantly, my thanks goes to *you*. Thank you for investing in yourself by taking the time to read this book. I hope you gain a ton of value out of it so that it's absolutely worth your time.

❝

Wealth is a
side effect of
financial literacy.

— *Kiana Danial*

About the Author

Kiana Danial, CEO of Invest Diva, is an award-winning, internationally recognized, personal-investing expert.

Featured in *The Wall Street Journal, TIME, Forbes, Kiplinger, Business Insider, TheStreet, Nasdaq, Fox Business, CNNi, Yahoo! Finance,* and *Cheddar,* Kiana is a highly sought-after commentator, professional speaker, and executive coach who has reported on the financial markets directly from the floor of the NYSE and NASDAQ. She won the Two Comma Club Award from ClickFunnels in 2021.

After dedicating two years to starting her business, perfecting her investment strategy, and writing her first book, which was published by McGraw-Hill, she opened a Tinder account in March 2014 and set her goal of finding a husband.

She had a clear vision about who she wanted him to be, his characteristics, and how he would make her feel. She even created a little jingle song about her vision that she would repeat to herself over and over again, which became her mantra.

While she was still working on managing her investment portfolio and growing her business, the most important steps had already been taken, so she had more time to go on dates. That's when she decided to dedicate her time to going on first dates.

This next part is super important:

She went on 397 first dates in three months.

Her rules for the first dates were:

- Nothing more than a coffee date.

- Not longer than an hour.

- Not getting upset if the guy was a douche.

- Try to look at it as learning something new.

ABOUT THE AUTHOR

This allowed her to meet a lot of men in a short period of time, and because they were back-to-back, she got to compare her prospects more logically without getting too emotional.

She met her husband on May 13, 2014. She says, "Because I had gone through so many 'frogs' back-to-back up to that point, it was a fairly easy decision to make."

They got married in March of 2015, on the Pi Day of the century 3/14/15, in a Pi-themed wedding:

https://investdiva.com/investing-guide/pi-day-wedding-how-far-can-two-geeks-go/

Since then, Kiana has written three more books, including the best-selling *Cryptocurrency Investing for Dummies*, published by Wiley in 2019, and the co-authored *Million Dollar Moms*,

195

which achieved #1 status on Amazon in eight different categories in 2020.

Kiana's mission with Invest Diva is to empower and educate women to take control of their financial future by investing in the online financial markets.

How to Get More Help

Building a legacy ... Making an impact ...
Creating a movement ...

These are a few reasons why I continue to work and what motivates our amazing Invest Diva Team on a daily basis.

I've seen how many people read my books, watch my educational TikTok/Instagram/YouTube videos, and even take my free classes. They get excited, feel empowered, and feel confident they can do it, and then they get in and they get stuck, frustrated, and consider giving up.

They're so close to getting to the next level. But they're frustrated with tiny little tactics that they forget about the process and give the whole thing up.

It breaks my heart because I know I can help them.

And that's why we're rapidly expanding our team to work closely with students who are ready to use the power of the Zen Wealth Generator to create generational wealth.

We will be working with select students who pass our application process. Is that you? Then visit:

MillionDollarFamily.org